TRIBUTE TO WORDSWORTH

WORDSWORTH

Drawn by John Buckland Wright
after a portrait by B. R. Haydon

TRIBUTE TO
WORDSWORTH

A MISCELLANY OF OPINION
FOR THE CENTENARY OF
THE POET'S DEATH

———

Foreword by HERBERT READ
Edited with Introductions by
MURIEL SPARK &
DEREK STANFORD

KENNIKAT PRESS
Port Washington, N. Y./London

TRIBUTE TO WORDSWORTH

First published in 1950
Reissued in 1970 by Kennikat Press
Library of Congress Catalog Card No: 73-113346
ISBN 0-8046-1035-5

Manufactured by Taylor Publishing Company   Dallas, Texas

FH

CONTENTS

HERBERT READ FOREWORD   *page* 9

MURIEL SPARK & DEREK STANFORD
Wordsworth the Person   13

WORDSWORTH AND HIS
NINETEENTH CENTURY CRITICS

S. T. COLERIDGE
From *To William Wordsworth*   21

DEREK STANFORD INTRODUCTION   23

Essays, Letters and Obiter Dicta :

WILLIAM HAZLITT   35

S. T. COLERIDGE   43

JOHN KEATS   57

THOMAS DE QUINCEY   59

WALTER BAGEHOT   71

THOMAS CARLYLE   75

JOHN STUART MILL   79

HENRI TAINE   83

WALTER PATER   87

MATTHEW ARNOLD   101

A. C. SWINBURNE   113

JAMES RUSSELL LOWELL   123

WORDSWORTH AND HIS
TWENTIETH CENTURY CRITICS

SIDNEY KEYES
  William Wordsworth   127

MURIEL SPARK INTRODUCTION   129

JOHN HEATH-STUBBS
  Wordsworth and Tradition   145

GEORGE WOODCOCK
  Wordsworth and the French Revolution   153

NORMAN NICHOLSON
  Wordsworth and the Lakes   161

G. S. FRASER
  Common Speech and Poetic Diction in Wordsworth   171

HENRY TREECE
  Wordsworth: His Impact and Influence   181

HERMANN PESCHMANN
  Wordsworth's Poetic Philosophy   191

WREY GARDINER
  Wordsworth's Prelude: A Verse Autobiography   205

ROBERT GREACEN
  Wordsworth as Politician   211

PATRICIA HUTCHINS
  Wordsworth's Prose   219

DEREK PATMORE
  Wordsworth and His Contemporaries   225

THE EDITORS desire to thank Messrs Routledge & Kegan Paul, Ltd, for the right to reproduce the poem *William Wordsworth* by Sidney Keyes; Messrs Heinemann Ltd, for permission to quote from Swinburne's essay *Byron and Wordsworth;* and also offer their sincere thanks to Mr H. K. Grant, Librarian of the Poetry Society, for his transcription of the nineteenth century extracts.

HERBERT READ

Foreword

LAST YEAR we celebrated the bi-centenary of Goethe's birth; this year we celebrate the centenary of Wordsworth's death. Both events have served to remind us that nothing is so difficult as to arrive at an objective judgment of a poet's work. His personality, attractive or repellent, is always there to exert magnetic influence on the workings of the critical mind.

In my own opinion we must accept this state of affairs. If an objective judgment means a judgment divorced from any consideration of the poet's social and economic circumstances, from his emotional and intellectual experiences, then it seems to me that though it may have interest as an academic exercise, it remains, as criticism, arid and unhelpful. We penetrate to the essence of a poet's work with the aid of two faculties – imagination and sympathy. I am willing to admit that imagination is most penetrating when least blurred by feeling, but for that very reason it is inadequate in a total act of appreciation. Appreciation requires sympathy – or, to be more exact and pedantic, empathy. By this we mean, not merely putting oneself in the poet's situation at the time he wrote the poem – that can be done by imagination. Rather we mean putting oneself in the poet's state of mind – thinking his thoughts, feeling his feelings, and thus understanding why he wrote in the particular way that he did write on a particular occasion. Only when we have indulged in this sympathetic identification with the poet are we in a position to exercise our judgment.

Admittedly the task in many cases is a difficult one. It may be made difficult, as in the case of Shakespeare, by the almost complete lack of evidence. But even in such a case, as Dr Ernest Jones has shown, the mysteries are not impenetrable. More baffling, perhaps, is the plethora of evidence present in a case such as Goethe's or Byron's. We are then apt to select the wrong facts to suit a pre-determined theory. In Wordsworth's case the facts are not too many and not too few. Dorothy's

Journal provides us with just those significant details which are so often absent; and in recent years what was hidden, to make matters so inexplicable, has been revealed. I do not propose to seize the unfair advantage of a Foreword to a symposium to defend my own interpretation of the facts of Wordsworth's life, but I would like to proclaim my sympathy, if not my partiality, for the poet. I do so because I think that this, in such a prominent place, is the example I should set.

That Wordsworth had a strain of harshness in his character is not to be denied, and it is made no more acceptable by being directed towards himself as well as towards others. The analytical explanation of such masochism would not be difficult. What is notable, however, is that this trait in his character did not seriously affect his relationships with his contemporaries. He must have been a difficult man to live with, but both Dorothy and Mary loved him deeply. When he was harsh with Coleridge, Coleridge was broken-hearted. Both Hazlitt and De Quincey write out of sympathy with him (and they were difficult men to please), and sensitive souls like Lamb and Keats had a warm affection for him. Only Carlyle strikes a discordant note, and in his case the lack of sympathy extends from the man to his work – 'his works I knew; but never considerably reverenced – could not, on attempting it'. But even Carlyle must admire the 'right good old steel-gray figure, with a fine rustic simplicity and dignity about him, and a veracious *strength* looking through him. . . .' The concession wrung from this unsympathetic critic is significant, for it is precisely this rusticity (not provincialism, but rooted autocthonous traditionalism) that constitutes the difficulty in the universal acceptance of Wordsworth's genius. Goethe's universality, Byron's cosmopolitanism – these are qualities that promote diffusion, even at the cost of confusion and misunderstanding. There can be no misunderstanding of Wordsworth, if only we are prepared to confront him on his own ground, which is the ground of a Cumberland 'statesman'. The deepest distinction implicit in Wordsworth's life and work is that between wisdom and sophistication – it is the basis not only of his philosophy, but also of his attitude to the craft of verse. Wordsworth realised that the best chance of finding and cultivating wisdom is among people who represent the oldest traditions in social life – among farmers and craftsmen producing and making the elementary necessities of life. They are the carriers of that tradition of meditation, older than the printed book, in which wisdom is condensed. Contact with that tradition, in Wordsworth's opinion, was the first necessity of a poet's life.

Even a hundred years is perhaps too short a time in which to discover whether Wordsworth was right or wrong. Civilisation, since his day, has not been on the side of simplicity! It might even be said that our sophisticated age demands a sophisticated form of art, and certainly there are no Wordsworths among us today. But our civilisation will soon pass away, and we may still say with De Quincey that 'meditative poetry is perhaps that province of literature which will ultimately maintain most power amongst the generations which are coming'. This is not meant as any disparagement of lyrical poetry, Wordsworth's least of all. A considerable number of his poems are accepted as 'pure' poetry even by dilettanti who are content to leave the *Prelude* and the *Excursion* unread. But Wordsworth's position as one of the half-dozen major English poets does not depend on his lyrical verse alone, or even principally. The specific virtue of Wordsworth was that, to adapt a phrase used by Keats in this connection, he thought with his heart, and *felt* the burden of the mystery. The tributes collected in this volume to the solace, illumination and ecstasy which he has thereby conferred, do not need any capping. But a younger generation has something to add to the chorus, for it has lived through times which have tested our values, and through which the poetry of Wordsworth has survived with undiminished appeal.

MURIEL SPARK

& DEREK STANFORD

Wordsworth the Person

WILLIAM WORDSWORTH died in the year of the Great Exhibition of 1850. Victorianism with its fug of profit had settled over the face of Britain, and beneath its pall a materialistic age was fast achieving its smoky prime. Wordsworth, who by now had become a Laureate whose function, it seemed, was largely to provide a rustic relaxation for the urban middle classes, had simultaneously rebuked and accepted the mercantile spirit of the age. For example, he had recently voiced his protest in a series of sonnets provoked by the construction of the Kendal-Windermere Railway, yet the whole tenor of his poetry, since Waterloo, had been to substantiate the *status quo*. How, one asks, was it possible for one of the greatest poets of our language, to decline into the particular state of atrophy which made an inglorious compromise inevitable? What were the elements in this man, that warred against his natural powers and internally sought to overcome him?

A penetrating statement by Wordsworth's comprehensive biographer, Professor Harper, more than any commentator save one, perhaps may give the clue to the poet's nature and the path this nature led him to take. He had, Professor Harper tells us, 'through almost lifelong association with gifted women, . . . a peculiar dependence upon womanly sympathy . . .' This observation Professor Harper develops towards a hypothesis which the present writers do not hold; the statement as such, however, is one that they feel provides the soundest starting point.

Mr Read, as is well known, has evolved a theory of his own on a somewhat similar basis; confining his examination of Wordsworth's dependence upon the feminine, to one particular person, she being the most significant. There were, none the less, three other women who deeply influenced the man and the poet, as well as a fourth whose image obsessed Wordsworth

[13]

long after he had ceased to write good poetry. Starting from Professor Harper's remark, we intend, in this essay, to suggest an extension of Mr Read's thesis; namely, that Wordsworth's life and work is best to be understood in the light of his relations to, firstly his mother, then to his early love, Annette Vallon; to his sister Dorothy, to his wife Mary and finally to his daughter, Dora.

As Wordsworth wrote (in Book V of the *Prelude*):

> Early died
> My honoured Mother, she who was the heart
> And hinge of all our learnings and our loves.

Sensing her presence, he saw nature through the veil of a warm and protective affection of which he speaks (in Book II):

> All that I now beheld
> Was dear to me, and from this cause it came,
> That now to Nature's finer influxes
> My mind lay open . . .

This early 'intercourse of touch' by which he 'held mute dialogues with [his] Mother's heart', gave him, according to Norman Lacey, a Mother-Ceres conception of landscape and a feeling of friendliness in natural elements.

The second woman in Wordsworth's development was the young Annette Vallon who liberated his erotic but inhibited instincts, endowing the poet with a later vision of nature tinged with remorse, guilt and tenderness. This early 'inheritance of blessedness' he was, after his desertion of Annette and the daughter of their union, to transfer to the Lakeland mountains, not without some melancholy colouring.

It was to his sister Dorothy that he turned for consolation and renewal after mutilating his own most powerful passion. In Dorothy he now found such source of peace and serenity as his nature was able to receive; and in his poem on Tintern Abbey, he refers to her as his 'dearest Friend', continuing:

> and in thy voice I catch
> The language of my former heart, and read
> My former pleasures in the shooting lights
> Of thy wild eyes. Oh! yet a little while
> May I behold in thee what I was once,
> My dear, dear Sister!

As the image of his mother was symbolised for him in the maternal face of nature, and as that of Annette created there a kind of erotic countenance, so Dorothy's image was projected in terms of contemplation and peace. This contemplation, and the poetry it produced were shared and encouraged by his sister; and in the poetry that sprang from Wordsworth's alliance with Dorothy, his perturbations and anxieties over Annette were imaginatively resolved, even though his feelings were still unsatisfied. His spiritual intimate, and, one might say, his most important reading public, were all combined in the person of Dorothy. It was due to her that nature seemed to wear a cheerful and affectionate expression, in between those visions of a deeper passion caused by the embodied memory of Annette.

In 1802 Wordsworth had made a final and decisive break with his long-neglected lover in France, and in the same year he married a friend of his school days, Mary Hutchinson, whose picture he has given us in one of his 'Lucy' poems. The poetic portrait of his bride is as flat as its subject was mild and domestic:

> She I cherished turned her wheel
> Beside an English fire.

However, the erotic tension which had returned with his loss of Annette was now channelised; though not perhaps focussed on an imaginatively stimulating subject. Annette seems to have stimulated both the physical and the erotic being; Dorothy inspired him and seems to have fulfilled his imaginative needs; Mary, however, appears only to have gratified the physical and social nature of the man.

From now on nature was invested with something of a tame and conventional temper. The poet who had formerly sought a place in the milieu of revolution or in the purlieus of 'rocks, and stones, and trees', now began to seek a more defined position in society. The rebel, the heretic, the 'half-atheist' thinker was fast adapting his attributes to the demands of orthodox opinion.

Now, since poetry is created out of conflict, tension, or a relationship which stimulates as much as it assuages, Wordsworth, we see, had lost by this marriage, the nervous substance vital to inspiration. For a while the presence of Dorothy perpetuated the condition necessary to his verse which he had known before marriage. Little by little, however, things were changing. An emotional displacement had taken place, and beside this loss of creative tension, there were other details encroaching upon him. Dorothy, writing of her brother in 1806, gives some indication of the poet's problems at this time. 'I cannot but admire,' she wrote, 'the fortitude, and wonder at the success, with which he has laboured in that one room, common to all the family, to all the visitors, and where the children frequently play beside him.' The fortitude may possibly have continued; the success attendant upon it diminished.

The fifth woman upon whom Wordsworth's thoughts and emotions came to be focussed, was Dora, the daughter of his marriage with Mary. Just as Dorothy in the past had played the rôle of amanuensis and poetic confidante – even for some time after his marriage – so in his later years it was Dora who accompanied her father on one of those tours of the Continent which the poet had enjoyed from time to time throughout his life. By now, however, he had ceased to discover in any one human person that stimulus which had illumined nature with its far-reaching rays. Dora, for whom her father's love was 'passionately jealous', as a friend of Wordsworth observed, was no longer able to inspire the poet, even though he was devoted to her to the point of being, as it was said, 'chicken-pecked'.

Wordsworth, then, seemed to require some profound emotional disturbance before the universe appeared to him in vital and imaginative terms. The source of this passionate vision in Wordsworth's life was Annette Vallon, whose image attracted and augmented the emotion he had once felt for his mother. Dorothy, with her own intense affection for him, perpetuated this responsiveness of the heart when the object that incited it was removed. With the advent of Mary, both the tension and the stimulus were lost. A low-voltage domestic feeling for his wife outwardly stabilised the man but inwardly assassinated the poet. That some half-conscious realisation of his emotional vacuum was probably present in him, we may assume from his attitude to Dora. Unable to call out his imagination as previous emotions had evoked it, his love for Dora may well be termed – as far as his poetry is concerned – a frustrate Pygmalion condition.

Wordsworth, as de Quincey remarked, was a man of 'strong animal passions'; and if his relationship with his daughter is of little significance to students of his poetry, the attitude adopted by him brings into relief other aspects of the man. Even considering the valuable evidence placed before us by the late Professor de Selincourt in his essay *Wordsworth and His Daughter's Marriage*, we must still incline to accept Professor Harper substantially when he says that 'for many years Wordsworth refused his consent to Dora's marriage, or gave it with such painful reluctance that it did not take place till 1841.' De Quincey, who knew both sides of Wordsworth, remarks that he was 'not generous; and not self-denying', and this avaricious obstinacy with regard to people and property is clearly manifest in the affair of Dora's procrastinated marriage.

Wordsworth was not an amiable person, and biographers who attempt to present him as such, are doing no service to an understanding, either of the man or of his works. The poet himself tells us that as a child he was 'stiff, moody, and of violent temper.' His mother said of him that he was the only one of her children about whom she felt anxiety, while de Quincey has reported that his nature was 'too stern and austere.' In his boyhood his pride and wilfulness led him on one occasion to an intention to kill himself, enraged at some fancied injury. Emerson, quoting Harriet Martineau, comments on the poet's parsimonious frugality in matters of housekeeping; and other of his contemporaries have spoken of his sparse and uncongenial speech, in the earlier period of his life – a further symptom of an inhibited and somewhat tight-fisted personality.

Prosperity, however enticed, when it came to Wordsworth, did not cause him to expand; and his friends noticed a touch of decay at the very inception of his better fortunes. Once more, we turn to his acquaintance de Quincey for an account of the poet's premature ageing, and how, in his fortieth year, Wordsworth was mistaken for a man of sixty.

The clawmark of the Eumenides, who had long pursued him,

now became visible. From his youth upward he had been haunted by fears of poverty and destitution. His sense of vocation as a poet having obsessed him from an early age, he was troubled by the question of how to secure an adequate means of following his art. His thoughts must often have been of:

> Cold, pain, and labour, and all fleshy ills;
> And mighty Poets in their misery dead.

This desire for independence led to selfishness from a concern lest his essential freedom be threatened in any way by circumstance; insecurity forced upon him a tyrannous stringency of outlook, to which his northern nature was susceptible.

It is as a victim, therefore, that we can best interpret Wordsworth the person. If his character and behaviour were such as not to endear him to others, and in certain cases to inflict suffering, he paid with the ultimate loss of his *raison d'être* as a human being; that is to say, with his poetic faculty. He had, after all, for more than a dozen years, produced some of the world's greatest poetry. From the start he possessed a deep recognition of spiritual phenomena, and so slight was his sense of outward reality that he himself recounted, 'I was often unable to think of external things as having external existence, and I communed with all that I saw as something not apart from, but inherent in, my own immaterial nature. Many times while going to school I have grasped a wall or tree to recall myself from this abyss of idealism to the reality.'

The idealism of which he speaks, Wordsworth did not employ outside of his poetry, until such time as he used it for coin to render to the Cæsar of his ethos. We well know in what coin he paid: Dorothy's journals attest to the increasing difficulty with which he composed as the years passed. The crown of the Laureate may be said to have rested on the brows of a man who figuratively had long since died. A writer capable of such expression as Wordsworth evinced at his prime, can never finally be satisfied, however prolific, in knowing his vision irrevocably departed.

A modern critic has said that 'no poem ever contradicts another poem, any more than one experience can be contradicted by another', and this has never been so pertinent as in the work of Wordsworth, in which the greatest of his literature is sufficient evidence to place in the balance against the tragedy of his premature decline.

For a compromising life, his apologia, as likewise our judgment upon him, remains implicit in his own statement:

> I made no vows, but vows
> Were then made for me; bond unknown to me
> Was given that I should be, else sinning greatly,
> A dedicated spirit.

WORDSWORTH AND HIS
NINETEENTH CENTURY CRITICS

Friend of the wise! and teacher of the good!
Into my heart have I received that lay
More than historic, that prophetic lay
Wherein (high theme by thee first sung aright)
Of the foundations and the building up
Of a Human Spirit, thou has dared to tell
What may be told, to the understanding mind
Revealable; and what within the mind,
By vital breathings secret as the soul
Of vernal growth, oft quickens in the heart
Thoughts all too deep for words!

S.T.COLERIDGE

From To William Wordsworth, *composed on the*
night after his recitation of a poem on the growth
of an individual mind

DEREK STANFORD

Introduction

'THIS WILL never do,' wrote Francis Jeffrey of Wordsworth's verse in 1814; a judgment which has since returned on the critic like an unskilfully handled boomerang. The reason for Jeffrey's negatory assertion need not trouble us today, for – as George Saintsbury remarks – 'a man who pronounces the *Daffodils* "stuff" puts himself down once for all, irrevocably without hope of pardon or of atonement, a person insensible to poetry as such.' Wordsworth, in the meantime, has 'done' very well. For over a hundred and fifty years, from the *Lyrical Ballads* in 1798, his poetry has proved how hard-wearing it is; how durably resistant to both the excesses of temporary belittlement or fulsome over-praise. Such extremes of opinion are now quite uncalled-for; and in the present symposium the editors have striven to harvest such homage as lies within the confines of good sense and taste.

Hazlitt, the first of our great critics to launch and advertise the poetry of Wordsworth, discovers much to commend and censure. As is generally the way with Hazlitt his judgments are suggested rather than stated. His assessments are all pictoria-lised, and the upshot of the whole matter is as inspiring and unmethodical as if one heard a High Court verdict delivered in the form of a prose poem. A writer, however, who flouts straight exposition and yet can still hit upon the following revelation must be allowed his own manner of working and find a respectful place in this collection. 'It is,' he writes of Words-worth's verse, 'as if there were nothing but himself and the universe. He lives in the busy solitude of his own heart.' This introspective self-absorption, resulting in the poet's deep but narrow appeal, is brilliantly described by the critic in his essay 'On Genius and Common Sense' (1821). 'Wordsworth,' he tells us, 'is the greatest, that is, the most original poet of the present day, only because he is the greatest egotist.' Hazlitt's chief declarations upon the poet, delivered in the course of three essays – ('On Mr Wordsworth's Excursion' [1817]; 'On the Living Poets' [1818]; and 'Mr Wordsworth' from *The Spirit of the Age* [1825]) – may be summarised as follows. Wordsworth did much to purify verse of a false rococo poeticism. By his example he helped to cleanse the Augean stables of late Augustan writing and restore to poetry its base of natural speech, upon which passion and imagination build. His fault, however, lay in trying to define this naturalness within a new norm; his quest for extreme simplicity ending in a fresh kind of artificial writing.

This theme – in a more systematic fashion – is taken up by Coleridge in Chapters XIV to XXII of his *Biographia Literaria* (1817). Wordsworthian criticism – criticism of the poet, that is, pursued as a form of reasoned enquiry rather than as some tiresome tirade or equally impossible panegyric; or, again, with Hazlitt in mind, as a pyrotechnic exercise or feat of fine writing – properly begins with Coleridge. Indeed, one may even go a step further and say that Wordsworth's poetry begins and ends with Coleridge likewise.

As Mr Middleton Murry observes in his book *The Mystery of Keats*, it was Coleridge who made 'the classical criticism' of Wordsworth's dogma of poetic diction. Classical is, perhaps, a strange word to apply to our greatest romantic critic; and if we erroneously take it to imply the cast-iron canons of Dr Johnson, its inappositeness forthwith becomes apparent. If, however, we incline to read it as synonymous with 'traditional' (meaning that which refers to and bears in mind the masterpieces of the past), then, the term is seen to fit Coleridge exactly, for such was his approach to Wordsworth's theoretics. But besides his historical sense of language, Coleridge was possessed of other faculties – feelings for the claims of consistency and reason – and these, in spite of tortuous thinking, speedily dispose of Wordsworth's doctrine. 'Were there excluded,' he writes (putting some eight chapters in a nutshell), 'from Mr Wordsworth's poetic compositions all that a literal adherence to the theory of his Preface would exclude, two thirds at least of the marked beauties of his poetry must be erased.'

Coleridge, none the less, was also the first critic methodically to account for the poet's merits, which – in the words of Saintsbury – he reduced to a 'high purity and appropriateness of language; weight and sanity of thoughts and sentiments; strength; originality and *curiosa felicitas* in single lines and paragraphs; truth of nature in imagery; meditative pathos; and, lastly, imagination in the highest and strictest sense of the word.'

A second critic who examines Wordsworth's theory of poetic diction from what we may call, in its largest sense, the traditional view-point is de Quincey. In his essay on the poet, five years before the Laureate's death in 1850, the argument which this critic employed was that of an appeal to the nature of our language. Rich in elements of Saxon and Latin, the English tongue, de Quincey maintained, could ill afford an austerity 'cut' in the name of some basically rustic speech. As he saw it, the Latin contribution provided us with our intellectual diction, whilst the Saxon constituent in our language guaranteed for us a vocabulary of feeling. Nor had any of our greatest poets recommended the expulsion of either of these parts. 'Spencer, Shakespeare, the Bible of 1611, and Milton – how say you, William Wordsworth' – de Quincey asks – 'are these sound and true as to diction, or are they not? If you say they *are*, then what is that you are proposing to change?'

De Quincey's critique has its positive side, too. As John Stuart Mill and Arnold were later to suggest, 'the distinction of Wordsworth, is the extent of his sympathy with what is really permanent in human feelings, and also the depth of this sympathy.' This permanency of pleasure, de Quincey derives from 'the truth of his love' of nature. The poetry of Wordsworth is something more than the lucubrations of botanist or tripper.

One quality, though, which Wordsworth did share with the naturalist was an eye for detail, an accurate perception of facts, a vivid and precise way of stating phenomena. This ocular realism on his part gives him certain affinities with the best of the Georgian and Imagist poets, and in his own day led Ruskin to praise his qualities as a foreground painter – 'the keenest-eyed of all modern poets for what is deep and essential in nature.' This higher exactitude in matters of description is further noted by George Henry Lewes, who, in his *Principles of*

Success in Literature (1865) contrasts a passage from Wordsworth's verse with one from Young's *Night Thoughts*, much to the advantage of the former. Wordsworth he examples as a poet who answers the need for distinct visual imagery; but remarks as well 'the marvellous clearness with which the whole scene is imagined, both in its objective and subjective relations – i.e. both in the objects seen and the emotions they suggest.'

This clear presentation of the eye's subject-matter has its corollary in the field of style. 'To Wordsworth,' wrote Walter Bagehot, in his essay on 'Wordsworth, Tennyson and Browning; or, Pure, Ornate, and Grotesque in English Poetry' (1864), 'To Wordsworth has been vouchsafed the last grace of the self-denying artist; you think neither of him nor his style, but you cannot help thinking of – you *must* recall – the exact phrase, the *very* sentiment he wished.' And of Wordsworth's sonnet 'Composed upon Westminster Bridge Sept 3rd 1802', he remarks: 'Instances of barer style than this may easily be found, instances of colder style – few better instances of purer style.' Wordsworth had certainly the chastest style, the most purely functional conception of language of all the English Romantic poets.

As to a sketch of Wordsworth the man – a pen-portrait of him by a contemporary – I have selected the one that Carlyle gives in his *Reminiscences*, which – written in 1867 – was the last work Carlyle attempted. The obvious alternatives to this choice are the three full-length sketches which de Quincey provides in his *Reminiscences of the Lake Poets* (1834–1839). Products of a greater and longer intimacy, these records of a shrewder, more orderly mind have been rejected on account of their fine deliberated malice. As with most of de Quincey's pen-drawings, we see the author at his game of cat-and-mouse with his subject. With one stroke he celebrates, and with the next he denigrates. The feline touch is always apparent, in statement or in counter-statement. This disqualifying gesture is one we do not discover in Carlyle. Whilst in no way wholeheartedly sympathetic, his memoir, we feel, is in large part disinterested (in so far as Carlyle can ever be that!). His 'Wordsworth', then, gives a picture of the poet seen by a mid-Victorian 'prophet'; and where the brushwork is least complimentary we perceive the difference in attitude between the mind of the Romantic Revival and that of the nineteenth century in all its provincial and self-assertive prime.

Nowhere better does this come out than in Carlyle's few patronising words about the intellectual theories of the poet. Wordsworth, he tells us, talked much of letters in a professional and technical way. He stuck close to vocables, avoiding things, and was 'joyfully reverent of the "wells of English undefiled"; though stone *dumb* as to the deeper rules, and wells of Eternal Truth and Harmony you were to try and set forth by said undefiled wells of English or what other speech you had!' Again, Carlyle notes how he reckoned Wordsworth's 'Poetic Storehouse to be far from an opulent or well furnished appartment', the 'divine reflections and unfathomabilities' of the poet seeming 'stinted, scanty; palish and uncertain; perhaps in part a feeble *reflex* . . . of the immense German fund of such?' Rhetorical and muddle-headed child, as Carlyle was, of imported German transcendentalism, he completely failed to understand how Wordsworth – influenced in his early days by the great empirical English thinkers, by the concrete and logical Hartley and Locke – had a certain kinship with the eighteenth century mind: its respect for boundaries, its suspicion of the infinite, its aversion towards talking of two subjects at once. In failing to understand Wordsworth, in fact, Carlyle shows himself, as a critic, without that sense of continuity – of evolution and tradition – without which any artistic judgment will always be largely irrelevant.

One of the finest 'personal testimonials' paid to the power of Wordsworth's verse is that which John Stuart Mill bestowed in his *Autobiography*, published in 1873. In the chapter 'One Stage Forward', he describes how a reading of the poet's verse affected a strange resurrection of his feelings, which for some time past had seemed atrophied or dead. A similar experiment with Byron's poetry had proved utterly useless, and it was only upon his perusing the shorter and miscellaneous pieces of Wordsworth that he felt a sense of hopeful pleasure once more stirring his mind and heart. The reason he gives for this awakening is as simple as the one that Arnold was to give some six years later in his essay on the poet. 'In the first place,' wrote the philosopher, speaking of his mental crisis in the year 1828, 'these poems addressed themselves to one of the strongest of my pleasurable susceptibilities, the love of rural objects and natural scenery ... I seemed to draw,' he continues, 'from a source of inward joy, of sympathetic and imaginative pleasures, which could be shared in by all human beings.'

This, we see, closely tallies with what Arnold was to describe as the ultimate source of the poet's greatness: 'Wordsworth's poetry is great because of the extraordinary power with which Wordsworth feels the joy offered to us in nature. . . . The source of joy from which he thus draws is the truest and most unfailing source of joy accessible to man. It is also accessible universally.'

Another tribute paid to the poet in the writings of John Stuart Mill occurs in his essay on *Poetry and its Varieties* published in 1859. Here, Wordsworth's verse is described as belonging to 'the poetry of culture' with which he contrasts the verse of Shelley, exemplifying spontaneous expression. By culture, in this context, is understood not the artificial as opposed to the natural, but rather a process of conscious maturation; of sowing, rearing, and harvesting one's thoughts. This, by the way, is an illustration of criticism's clarifying redundance; for Wordsworth himself had suggested as much when he spoke of waiting for inspiration in a kind of 'wise passiveness' and of his moment of composition as one of 'emotion recollected in tranquillity.'

From the Gallic viewpoint, a second critic who failed to understand rightly Wordsworth was the hard and brilliant positivist, Taine. Formed himself by methods of study most rigorous and scientific, he proved unable to recognise the poetic reasoning of Wordsworth's verse. Finding, once more, a German influence, when the strongest were those of Hartley and Locke, and – as for most English Romantics – the inevitable fathering spirit of Plato, Taine serves to illustrate how Wordsworth is a poet peculiar and accessible to the Anglo-Saxon intelligence alone. A misty mountain seen from a laboratory window; a beauty somewhat useless and removed – such is Taine's first impression of Wordsworth, whose sermonising landscapes again repelled the critic.

Sainte-Beuve, it is true, who criticises Taine for not alloting a rightful place to the poets of the Lakes, mentions Wordsworth always with respect, and writes a most sympathetic study of Cowper whom he regarded as the former's baptist. In the absence of essays upon Wordsworth by Renan and de Gourmont, we are, therefore, reproducing Taine's.

Another writer who somewhat tended to look at Wordsworth from the townee view-point was the banker-critic, Walter Bagehot – brilliant defender of 'animated moderation'. Wordsworth, he suggests in an article on Hartley Coleridge (1852) was the author of a kind of natural Bible; but the Scriptures he gives, opines the critic, are apt to fall between the stools of humanity's two most common needs. 'What active men require,' Bagehot tells us, 'is personality; the meditative require beauty. But Wordsworth gives us neither.' None the less, he recognises the nourishment that the poet imparts to 'the solitary and the young'; and in his essay (1855) on *The First Edinburgh Reviewers*, although appreciating Jeffrey's position, defends the poet's unspecified mysticism against the literal-mindedness of the Whig dictator.

A by no means insignificant element within the body of Wordsworthian opinion is that contributed by the nineteenth century poets. Pertinent, confused, and often contradictory, the remarks made on Wordsworth by other poets are instructive, revealing, and entertaining reading. Shelley, for example, who fantastically observes that Wordsworth 'had no more imagination than a pint pot', concedes to him 'a sort of sense in thought'. Byron, as usual, is uncomplimentary. Browning, following in the footsteps of Shelley, describes his last phase as *'pulvis et cinis'*. Darley writes of him as 'Old Wordy', and laughs at his *'Simpletonian* system'; whilst Leight Hunt, less unjustly, calls him 'a kind of puritan retainer of the Establishment'. But by far the fairest and most perspicacious account delivered by the poets themselves on Wordsworth is that which we find in the letters of Keats (see, chiefly, two to his friend Reynolds, February 3rd, and May 3rd 1818). The substance of Keats' reaction may be described as a conflict between his aversion towards the poet's nominal system and his sense of Wordsworth's deeper inner wisdom; an opposition which Mr Middleton Murry, in his book *The Mystery of Keats*, has tried to show was at length resolved.

A somewhat less valuable body of opinion concerning the merits and nature of the poet was that compiled by the Wordsworthians – 'the devout Wordsworthians', as Arnold describes them. This term is not to be taken as limited in its application to any specific group of authors, but as referring to those fans and critics who found in Wordsworth a paragon of poetic virtue, outside of all comparison. One of them, Henry Taylor, maintained that the style of his idol was even superior to that of Aeschylus, Shakespeare, or Milton; whilst the band of faithful followers, as a whole, were not content with relegating to him the highest poetic excellence, but needs must proclaim him the one true repository of philosophic wisdom in their day.

The only one of these in any way able to substantiate, as well as to moderate, his claim, was the Utilitarian, Leslie Stephens, whose essay on Wordsworth is a brilliant though possibly irrelevant document. The essence of Stephens' argument is that the poet attempted to reconcile the childhood instincts of natural harmony with the moral precepts of adulthood. These early intimations the critics equated with the racial memory of the anthropologists, attempting to establish a scientific basis for Wordsworth's doctrine of natural piety.

In 1879 there appeared Arnold's volume of selections from the poet; an event of much occasion in the course of Wordsworthian opinion. De Quincey, John Stuart Mill, and Pater had all to some extent anticipated him; but none had said so forcefully and clearly what Arnold now himself maintained. Gently laughing at the Wordsworthians for their muddled earnestness concerning the message to be got from the poet, Arnold, without any further ado, proceeds to assert categorically that 'poetry is the reality, philosophy the illusion'. But if Arnold warns us against approaching Wordsworth for the sake of some philosophy or other, he does not wish us to view the poet in any purely æsthetic light. Wordsworth, he tells us, is a poet of ideas, and his poetry offers 'a criticism of life'. What quite Arnold meant by this, many critics have variously striven to explain. In so far as by ideas we imply a talk of generalisations, the formulation of personal experience in profoundly reflective terms, then Wordsworth, we can say, is an intellectual poet. This 'ideational' element in Wordsworth is something that our present-day critics – Mr Herbert Read and Mr Middleton Murry, above all – have been at some pains to define; and Muriel Spark, in her introduction to the second section of this volume has some pertinent words to say about them.

Pater's essay, written some five years before Arnold's, in many ways prefigures the latter's conclusions. Reacting from the orthodox Wordsworthians, Pater would have us resort to the poet not for any 'home-made' philosophy of nature but for an increase in sensibility – an augmented awareness to the life of landscape and to the life of man within it. Concerning Words-worth's abstract thinking, he notes, it is true, 'the fascination of bold speculative ideas' in the poet, but suggests that they are used 'with a very fine apprehension of the limits within which alone philosophical imaginings have any place in true poetry' It is, indeed, to an 'exceptional susceptibility to the impressions of ear and eye'; to what, in the long run, was 'a kind of sen-suousness', that Pater reduced Wordsworth's pantheism. All that is really left after the critic's delicate disinfection, is a landscape 'ennobled by a semblance of passion and thought' – a suggestive rather than a mystical universe. Pater persuades us, then, to see in Wordsworth's verse not a spiritual but a subjective nature; a nature, saturated, so to speak, in anthropocentric colouring. It is, therefore, the fraternal likeness, and not the alien 'otherness' which Pater finds in the landscapes of the poet. In Wordsworth, man and nature are of the same species.

In much that Wordsworth said, wrote the critic, speaking of the poet's Prefaces – 'he was but pleading indirectly for that sincerity, that perfect fidelity to one's own inward presentations, to the precise features of the picture within, without which any profound poetry is impossible.' Thus, by the gentlest of argu-ments, by his courteous, shy, and slow-moving prose, Pater relieves the poet of his more purposeful attributes. He detects, for example, a Platonic aberration – 'the old heresy of Origen' – present in the poet's great Ode on childhood; and notes how Wordsworth's imaginative findings are often at variance with the dogmas of the man. Wordsworth, he feels, must not be read by the regulation candle of orthodoxy. Not religion, but a working of the religious instinct; not an ethic, but reflections on the nature of man: such, suggests Pater, is what the poet offers. 'Contemplation – impassioned contemplation – that is, with Wordsworth the end-in-itself.'

Father of the English Symbolist school, Pater sought always, in literature, for a rarefied distillation of expression, an intense quintessential employment of speech. To lighten Wordsworth of all his humdrum: his surplus of uninspired writing was an end which Pater bore in mind. 'Of all poets equally great,' wrote the critic, 'he would gain most by a skilfully made anthology.' This concentration on the æsthetic aspect of Wordsworth's poetry by Pater is a fact of much significance. For every thousand readers who delight in *Lucy Gray*, *Daffodils*, and *The Green Linnet*, not more than one, perhaps, today, is concerned with Wordsworth's philosophic system. That Wordsworth – whatever view we take, and however we incline to discount his 'message' – must still be reckoned a very great poet: such, on the whole, is our present feeling – a position which Pater did much to develop.

Following in the track of Arnold and Pater, though with that excitable independence informing all his critical writings, comes Swinburne with his pronouncement on the poet. Wordsworth, he argues – repudiating Arnold – merits our deep attention and respect not because his verse incapsulates any 'criticism of life', but because, in his felicitous handling of speech, he manifests the two most high poetic virtues of 'harmony and imagination'. Focussing his interest on the poet's verbal structure, more than any critic since Coleridge had done, Swinburne rather surprisingly states that Wordsworth's distinction as a poet is not in his use of natural language but in his control of elevated speech. He is the poet of the 'tender sublime': this is Swinburne's case, and one argued most convincingly.

A third nineteenth century critic whose chief concern with Wordsworth was his usage of language is the American, James Russell Lowell; and his essay (1875) upon the poet – as Professor Garrod has pointed out – is probably the most balanced of Wordsworthian assessments. It is certainly – of all – the most charmingly written.

One final critic deserving a mention is Stopford A. Brook whose literary sermons – *Theology in the English Poets* – were first delivered in 1872 from the pulpit of St James's Chapel before publication in 1874. Half of the pages of this still interesting work are devoted to what the critic termed Wordsworth's 'theology in the raw'. The writer, later, became a Unitarian.

Voice of a century of free enterprise, of narrow unchecked individualism, Victorian criticism, on the whole, is even more 'unplanned' and desultory than our own. In its animadversions on the poet, however, we find certain aspects more to the fore, receiving a lion's share of attention. These were: Wordsworth's theory of diction, the language of his poems, and, finally, his 'moral' and his 'message'. What factor in Wordsworth attracts our own time, and the way our critics have approached that factor, is the subject of my colleague's introduction to the second section of this book.

HAZLITT

1

MR WORDSWORTH's genius is a pure emanation of the Spirit of the Age. Had he lived in any other period of the world, he would never have been heard of. As it is, he has some difficulty to contend with the hebetude of his intellect, and the meanness of his subject. With him 'lowliness is young ambition's ladder': but he finds it a toil to climb in this way the steep of Fame. His homely Muse can hardly raise her wing from the ground, nor spread her hidden glories to the sun. He has 'no figures nor no fantasies, which busy *passion* draws in the brains of men': neither the gorgeous machinery of mythologic lore, nor the splendid colours of poetic diction. His style is vernacular: he delivers household truths. He sees nothing loftier than human hopes; nothing deeper than the human heart. This he probes, this he tampers with, this he poises, with all its incalculable weight of thought and feeling, in his hands; and at the same time calms the throbbing pulses of his own heart, by keeping his eye ever fixed on the face of nature. If he can make the lifeblood flow from the wounded breast, this is the living colouring with which he paints his verse: if he can assuage the pain or close up the wound with the balm of solitary musing, or the healing power of plants and herbs and 'skyey influences', this is the sole triumph of his art. He takes the simplest elements of nature and of the human mind, the mere abstract conditions inseparable from our being, and tries to compound a new system of poetry from them; and has perhaps succeeded as well as any one could. '*Nihil humani a me alienum puto*' – is the motto of his works. He thinks nothing low or indifferent of which this can be affirmed: every thing that professes to be more than this, that is not an absolute essence of truth and feeling, he holds to be vitiated, false, and spurious. In a word, his poetry is founded on setting up an opposition (and pushing it to the utmost length) between the natural and the artificial; between the spirit of humanity, and the spirit of fashion and of the world!

It is one of the innovations of the time. It partakes of, and is carried along with, the revolutionary movement of our age: the political changes of the day were the model on which he formed and conducted his poetical experiments. His Muse (it cannot be denied, and without this we cannot explain its character at all) is a levelling one. It proceeds on a principle of equality, and strives to reduce all things to the same standard. It is distinguished by a proud humility. It relies upon its own resources, and disdains external show and relief. It takes the commonest events and objects, as a test to prove that nature is always interesting from its inherent truth and beauty, without any of the ornaments of dress or pomp of circumstances to set it off. Hence the unaccountable mixture of seeming simplicity and real abstruseness in the *Lyrical Ballads*. Fools have laughed at, wise men scarcely understood them. He takes a subject or a story merely as pegs or loops to hang thought and feeling on; the incidents are trifling, in proportion to his contempt for imposing appearances; the reflections are profound, according to the gravity and the aspiring pretensions of his mind.

His popular, inartificial style gets rid (at a blow) of all the trappings of verse, of all the high places of poetry: 'the cloud-capt towers, the solemn temples, the gorgeous palaces', are swept to the ground, and 'like the baseless fabric of a vision, leave not a wreck behind'. All the traditions of learning, all the superstitions of age, are obliterated and effaced. We begin *de novo*, on a *tabula rasa* of poetry. The purple pall, the nodding plume of tragedy are exploded as mere pantomime and trick, to return to the simplicity of truth and nature. Kings, queens, priests, nobles, the altar and the throne, the distinctions of rank, birth, wealth, power, 'the judge's robe, the marshal's truncheon, the ceremony that to great ones 'longs', are not to be found here. The author tramples on the pride of art with greater pride. The Ode and Epode, the Strophe and the Antistrophe, he laughs to scorn. The harp of Homer, the trump of Pindar and of Alcaeus are still. The decencies of costume, the decorations of vanity are stripped off without mercy as barbarous, idle, and Gothic. The jewels in the crisped hair, the diadem on the polished brow are thought meretricious, theatrical, vulgar; and nothing contents his fastidious taste beyond a simple garland of flowers.

Neither does he avail himself of the advantages which nature or accident holds out to him. He chooses to have his subject a foil to his inventions, to owe nothing but to himself. He gathers manna in the wilderness, he strikes the barren rock for the gushing moisture. He elevates the mean by the strength of his own aspirations; he clothes the naked with beauty and grandeur from the stores of his own recollections. No cypress grove loads his verse with funeral pomp: but his imagination leads a sense of joy:

> To the bare trees and mountains bare,
> And grass in the green field.

No storm, no shipwreck startles us by its horrors: but the rainbow lifts its head in the cloud, and the breeze sighs through the withered fern. No sad vicissitude of fate, no overwhelming catastrophe in nature deforms his page: but the dew-drop glitters on the bending flower, the tear collects in the glistening eye:

> Beneath the hills, along the flowery vales,
> The generations are prepared; the pangs,
> The internal pangs are ready; the dread strife
> Of poor humanity's afflicted will,
> Struggling in vain with ruthless destiny.

As the lark ascends from its low bed on fluttering wing, and salutes the morning skies; so Mr Wordsworth's unpretending Muse, in russet guise, scales the summits of reflection, while it makes the round earth its footstool, and its home!

Possibly a good deal of this may be regarded as the effect of disappointed views and an inverted ambition. Prevented by native pride and indolence from climbing the ascent of learning or greatness, taught by political opinions to say to the vain pomp and glory of the world, 'I hate ye', seeing the path of classical and artificial poetry blocked up by the cumbrous ornaments of style and turgid *common-places*, so that nothing more could be achieved in that direction but by the most ridiculous bombast or the tamest servility; he has turned back partly from the bias of his mind, partly perhaps from a judicious policy – has struck into the sequestered vale of humble life, sought out the Muse among sheep-cotes and hamlets and the peasants' mountain-haunts, has discarded all the tinsel pageantry of verse, and, endeavoured (not in vain) to aggrandise the trivial and add the charm of novelty to the familiar. No one has shown the same imagination in raising trifles into importance: no one has displayed the same pathos in treating of the simplest feelings of the heart. Reserved, yet haughty, having no unruly or violent passions, (or those passions having been early suppressed,) Mr Wordsworth has passed his life in solitary musing, or in daily converse with the face of nature. He exemplifies in an eminent degree the power of association; for his poetry has no other source or character. He has dwelt among pastoral scenes, till each object has become connected with a thousand feelings, a link in the chain of thought, a fibre of his own heart. Every one is by habit, and familiarity strongly attached to the place of his birth, or to objects that recall the most pleasing and eventful circumstances of his life. But to the author of the *Lyrical Ballads*, nature is a kind of home; and he may be said to take a personal interest in the universe. There is no image so insignificant that it has not in some mood or other found the way into his heart: no sound that does not awaken the memory of other years.

> To him the meanest flower that blows can give
> Thoughts that do often lie too deep for tears.

The daisy looks up to him with sparkling eye as an old acquaintance: the cuckoo haunts him with sounds of early youth not to be expressed: a linnet's nest startles him with boyish delight: an old withered thorn is weighed down with a heap of recollections: a grey cloak, seen on some wild moor, torn by the wind, or drenched in the rain, afterwards becomes an object of imagination to him: even the lichens on the rock have a life and being in his thoughts. He has described all these objects in a way and with an intensity of feeling that no one else had done before him, and has given a new view or aspect of nature. He is in this sense the most original poet now living, and the one whose writings could the least be spared: for they have no substitute elsewhere. The vulgar do not read them, the learned, who see all things through books, do not understand them, the great despise, the fashionable may ridicule them: but the author has created himself an interest in the heart of the retired and lonely student of nature, which can never die. Persons of this class will still continue to feel what he has felt: he has expressed what they might in vain wish to express, except with glistening eye and faultering [sic] tongue! There is a lofty philosophic tone, a thoughtful humanity, infused into his pastoral vein. Remote from the passions and events of the great world, he has communicated interest and dignity to the primal movements of the heart of man, and ingrafted his own conscious reflections on the casual thoughts of hinds and shepherds. Nursed amidst the grandeur of mountain scenery, he has stooped to have a nearer view of the daisy under his feet, or plucked a branch of white-thorn from the spray: but in describing it, his mind seems imbued with the majesty and solemnity of the objects around him – the tall rock lifts its head in the erectness of his spirit; the cataract roars in the sound of his verse; and in its dim and mysterious meaning, the mists seem to gather in the hollows of Helvellyn, and the forked Skiddaw hovers in the distance. There is little mention of mountainous scenery in Mr Wordsworth's poetry; but by internal evidence one might be almost sure that it was written in a mountainous country, from its bareness, its simplicity, its loftiness and its depth. . . .

[The Spirit of the Age and English Poets]

2

MR WORDSWORTH is the most original poet now living. He is the reverse of Walter Scott in his defects and excellences. He has nearly all that the other wants, and wants all that the other possesses. His poetry is not external, but internal; it does not depend upon tradition, or story, or old song, he furnishes it from his own mind, and is his own subject. He is the poet of mere sentiment. Of many of the *Lyrical Ballads*, it is not possible to speak in terms of too high praise, such as *Hart-leap Well*, *The Banks of the Wye*, *Poor Susan*, parts of *The Leech-gatherer*, the *Lines to a Cuckoo*, *To a Daisy*, *The Complaint*, several of the sonnets, and a hundred others of inconceivable beauty, of perfect originality and pathos. They open a finer and deeper vein of thought and feeling than any poet in modern times has done, or attempted. He has produced a deeper impression, and on a smaller circle, than any other of his contemporaries. His powers have been mistaken by the age, nor does he exactly understand them himself. He cannot form a whole. He has not the constructive faculty. He can give only the fine tones of thought, drawn from his mind by accident or nature, like the sounds drawn from the Æolian harp by the wandering gale. He is totally deficient in all the machinery of poetry. His *Excursion*, taken as a whole, notwithstanding the noble materials thrown away in it, is a proof of this. The line labours, the sentiment moves slow, but the poem stands stock-still. The reader makes no way from the first line to the last. It is more than anything in the world like Robinson Crusoe's boat, which would have been an excellent good boat, and would have carried him to the other side of the globe, but that he could not get it out of the sand where it stuck fast. I did what little I could to help to launch it at the time, but it would not do. I am not, however, one of those who laugh at the attempts or failures of men of genius. It is not my way to cry 'Long life to the conqueror'. Success and desert are not with me synonymous terms; and the less Mr Wordsworth's general merits have been understood, the more necessary is it to insist upon them . . .

[*On the Living Poets*]

3

IN POWER of intellect, in lofty conception, in the depth of feeling, at once simple and sublime, which pervades every part of it, and which gives to every object an almost preternatural and preterhuman interest, this work has seldom been surpassed. The poem of *The Excursion* resembles that part of the country in which the scene is laid. It has the same vastness and magnificence, with the same nakedness and confusion. It has the same overwhelming, oppressive power. It excites or recalls the same sensations which those who have traversed that wonderful scenery must have felt. We are surrounded with the constant sense and superstitious awe of the collective power of matter, of the gigantic and eternal forms of nature, on which, from the beginning of time, the hand of man has made no impression. Here are no dotted lines, no gravel walks, no square mechanic inclosures; all is left loose and irregular in the rude chaos of aboriginal nature. The boundaries of hill and valley are the poet's only geography, where we wander with him incessantly over deep beds of moss and waving fern, amidst the troops of red-deer and wild animals. Such is the severe simplicity of Mr Wordsworth's taste that I doubt whether he would not reject a druidical temple, or time-hallowed ruin, as too modern and artificial for his purpose. He only familiarises himself or his readers with a stone, covered with lichens, which has slept in the same spot of ground from the creation of the world, or with the rocky fissure between two mountains caused by thunder, or with a cavern scooped out by the sea. His mind is, as it were, coeval with the primary forms of things; his imagination holds immediately from nature, and 'owes no allegiance' but 'to the elements'.

The Excursion may be considered as a philosophical pastoral poem, as a scholastic romance. It is less a poem on the country than on the love of the country. It is not so much a description of natural objects as of the feelings associated with them; not an account of the manners of rural life, but the result of the poet's reflections on it. He does not present the reader with a lively succession of images or incidents, but paints the outgoings of his own heart, the shapings of his own fancy. He may be said to create his own materials; his thoughts are his real subject. His understanding broods over that which is 'without form and void', and 'makes it pregnant'. He sees all things in himself. He hardly ever avails himself of remarkable objects or situations, but, in general, rejects them as interfering with the workings of his own mind as disturbing the smooth, deep, majestic current of his own feelings. Thus his descriptions of natural scenery are not brought home distinctly to the naked eye by forms and circumstances, but every object is seen through the medium of innumerable recollections, is clothed with the haze of imagination like a glittering vapour, is obscured with the excess of glory, has the shadowy brightness of a waking dream. The image is lost in the sentiment, as sound in the multiplication of echoes:

> And visions, as prophetic eyes avow,
> Hang on each leaf, and cling to every bough.

In describing human nature, Mr Wordsworth equally shuns the common 'vantage-grounds of popular story, of striking incident, or fatal catastrophe, as cheap and vulgar modes of producing an effect. He scans the human race as the naturalist measures the earth's zone, without attending to the picturesque points of view, the abrupt inequalities of surface. He contemplates the passions and habits of men, not in their extremes, but in the first elements; their follies and vices, not at their height, with all their embossed evils upon their heads, but as lurking in embryo, the seeds of the disorder inwoven with our very constitution. He only sympathises with those simple forms of feeling which mingle at once with his own identity, or with the stream of general humanity. To him the great and the small are the same; the near and the remote; what appears, and what only is. The general and the permanent, like the Platonic ideas, are his only realities. All accidental varieties and individual contrasts are lost in an endless continuity of feeling; like drops of water in the ocean-stream! An intense intellectual egotism swallows up everything. Even the dialogues introduced in the present volume are soliloquies of the same character, taking different views of the subject. The recluse, the pastor, and the pedlar, are three persons in one poet. I myself disapprove of these 'interlocutions between Lucius and Caius' as impertinent babbling, where there is no dramatic distinction of character. But the evident scope and tendency of Mr Wordsworth's mind is the reverse of dramatic. It resists all change of character, all variety of scenery, all the bustle, machinery, and pantomime of the stage, or of real life, whatever might relieve, or relax, or change the direction of its own activity, jealous of all competition. The power of his mind preys upon itself. It is as if there were nothing but himself and the universe. He lives in the busy solitude of his own heart; in the deep silence of thought. His imagination lends life and feeling only to 'the bare trees and mountains bare'; peoples the viewless tracts of air, and converses with the silent clouds!

[*On Mr Wordsworth's* Excursion]

COLERIDGE

WORDSWORTH, where he is indeed Wordsworth, may be mimicked by copyists, he may be plundered by plagiarists; but he cannot be imitated except by those who are not born to be imitators. For without his depth of feeling and his imaginative power, his sense would want its vital warmth and peculiarity; and without his strong sense, his mysticism would become sickly – mere fog, and dimness!

To . . . defects which . . . are only occasional, I may oppose with far less fear of encountering the dissent of any candid and intelligent reader, the following (for the most part correspondent) excellences. First, an austere purity of language both grammatically and logically; in short a perfect appropriateness of the words to the meaning. Of how high value I deem this, and how particularly estimable I hold the example at the present day, has been already stated: and in part too the reasons on which I ground both the moral and intellectual importance of habituating ourselves to a strict accuracy of expression. It is noticeable, how limited an acquaintance with the masterpieces of art will suffice to form a correct and even a sensitive taste, where none but masterpieces have been seen and admired: while on the other hand, the most correct notions, and the widest acquaintance with the works of excellence of all ages and countries, will not perfectly secure us against the contagious familiarity with the far more numerous offspring of tastelessness or of a perverted taste. If this be the case, as it notoriously is, with the arts of music and painting, much more difficult will it be, to avoid the infection of multiplied and daily examples in the practice of an art, which uses words, and words only, as its instruments. In poetry, in which every line, every phrase, may pass the ordeal of deliberation and deliberate choice, it is possible, and barely possible, to attain that *ultimatum* which I have ventured to propose as the infallible test of a blameless style, namely, its untranslatableness in words of the same language without injury to the meaning. Be it observed, however, that I include in the meaning of a word not only its correspondent object, but likewise all the associations which it recalls. For language is framed to convey not the object alone, but likewise the character, mood and intentions of the person who is representing it. In poetry it is practicable to preserve the diction uncorrupted by the affectations and misappropriations, which promiscuous authorship, and reading not promiscuous only because it is disproportionally most conversant with the compositions of the day, have rendered general. Yet even to the poet, composing in his own province, it is an arduous work: and as the result and pledge of a watchful good sense, of fine and luminous distinction, and of complete self-possession, may justly claim all the honour which belongs to an attainment equally difficult and valuable, and the more valuable for being rare. It is at all times the proper food of the understanding; but in an age of corrupt eloquence it is both food and antidote.

The second characteristic excellence of Mr Wordsworth's works is: a correspondent weight and sanity of the thoughts and sentiments, – won, not from books, but – from the poet's own meditative observation. They are fresh, and have the dew upon them. His muse, at least when in her strength of wing, and when she hovers aloft in her proper element:

> Makes audible a linked lay of truth,
> Of truth profound a sweet continuous lay,
> Not learnt, but native, her own natural notes!
>
> (*S. T. C.*)

Even throughout his smaller poems there is scarcely one, which is not rendered valuable by some just and original reflection.

See *Star Gazers:* or the two following passages in one of his humblest compositions:

> O Reader! had you in your mind
> Such stores as silent thought can bring,
> O gentle Reader! you would find
> A tale in every thing.

and

I have heard of hearts unkind, kind deeds
With coldness still returning:
Alas! the gratitude of men
Has oftener left me mourning.'

Simon Lee

Or in a still higher strain the six beautiful quatrains (*The Fountain*):

Thus fares it still in our decay:
And yet the wiser mind
Mourns less for what age takes away
Than what it leaves behind.

The Blackbird in the summer trees,
The Lark upon the hill,
Let loose their carols when they please,
Are quiet when they will.

With Nature never do *they* wage
A foolish strife: they see
A happy youth, and their old age
Is beautiful and free!

But we are pressed by heavy laws
And often, glad no more,
We wear a face of joy, because
We have been glad of yore.

If there is one, who need bemoan
His kindred laid in earth.
The household hearts that were his own
It is the man of mirth.

My days, my Friend, are almost gone,
My life has been approved,
And many love me; but by none
Am I enough beloved.

or the Sonnet on Buonaparte; or finally (for a volume would scarce suffice to exhaust the instances), the last stanza of the poem on *The Withered Celandine*:

To be a prodigal's favourite – then, worse truth,
A miser's pensioner – behold our lot!
O man! that from thy fair and shining youth
Age might but take the things youth needed not.

Both in respect of this and of the former excellence, Mr Words-
worth strikingly resembles Samuel Daniel, one of the golden
writers of our golden Elizabethan age, now most causelessly
neglected: Samuel Daniel, whose diction bears no mark of time,
no distinction of age, which has been, and as long as our language
shall last will be, so far the language of the today and for ever,
as that it is more intelligible to us, than the transitory fashions
of our own particular age. A similar praise is due to his senti-
ments. No frequency of perusal can deprive them of their fresh-
ness. For though they are brought into the full daylight of every
reader's comprehension, yet are they drawn up from depths
which few in any age are privileged to visit, into which few in
any age have courage or inclination to descend. If Mr Words-
worth is not equally with Daniel alike intelligible to all readers
of average understanding in all passages of his works, the
comparative difficulty does not arise from the greater impurity
of the ore, but from the nature and uses of the metal. A poem
is not necessarily obscure, because it does not aim to be popular.
It is enough, if a work be perspicuous to those for whom it is
written, and:

Fit audience find, though few.

To the *Ode on the Intimations of Immortality from Recollections
of early Childhood* the poet might have prefixed the lines which
Dante addresses to one of his own *Canzoni*:

*Canzon, io credo, che saranno radi
Che tua ragione intendan bene:
Tanto lor sei faticoso ed alto.*

O lyric song, there will be few, think I,
Who may thy import understand aright:
Thou art for *them* so arduous and so high!

But the ode was intended for such readers only as had been
accustomed to watch the flux and reflux of their inmost nature,

to venture at times into the twilight realms of consciousness,
and to feel a deep interest in modes of inmost being, to which
they know that the attributes of time and space are inapplicable
and alien, but which yet cannot be conveyed, save in symbols
of time and space. For such readers the sense is sufficiently plain,
and they will be as little disposed to charge Mr Wordsworth
with believing the platonic pre-existence in the ordinary inter-
pretation of the words, as I am to believe, that Plato himself
ever meant or taught it:

—πολλά μοι ὑπ' ἀ γκῶ
—νος ὠκέα βέλη
ἔνδον ἐντι φαρέτρας
φωνᾶντα συνετοῖσιν' ἐς
δὲ τὸ πᾶν ἐρμηνέων
χατίζει. σοφὸς ὁ πολ
—λα εἰδὼς φυᾷ
μαθόντες δὲ λάβροι
παγλωσσίᾳ, κορακες ὢς
ἄκραντα γαρύετον
Διὸς πρὸς ὄρνιχα θεῖον

Third (and wherein he soars far above Daniel) the sinewy
strength and originality of single lines and paragraphs: the
frequent *curiosa felicitas* of his diction, of which I need not here
give specimens, having anticipated them in a preceding page.
This beauty, and as eminently characteristic of Wordsworth's
poetry, his rudest assailants have felt themselves compelled to
acknowledge and admire.

Fourth; the perfect truth of nature in his images and descrip-
tions as taken immediately from nature, and proving a long and
genial intimacy with the very spirit which gives the physio-
gnomic expression to all the works of nature. Like a green field
reflected in a calm and perfectly transparent lake, the image is
distinguished from the reality only by its greater softness and
lustre. Like the moisture or the polish on a pebble, genius
neither distorts nor false-colours its objects; but on the contrary
brings out many a vein and many a tint, which escape the eye of
common observation, thus raising to the rank of gems what had
been often kicked away by the hurrying foot of the traveller on
the dusty highroad of custom.

Let me refer to the whole description of skating (*Influence of Natural Objects*), especially to the lines:

> So through the darkness and the cold we flew
> And not a voice was idle: with the din
> Meanwhile the precipices rang aloud;
> The leafless trees and every icy crag
> Tinkled like iron; while the distant hills
> Into the tumult sent an alien sound
> Of melancholy, not unnoticed, while the stars
> Eastward were sparkling clear, and in the west
> The orange sky of evening died away.

Or to the poem on *The Green Linnet*. What can be more accurate yet more lovely than the two concluding stanzas?

> Upon yon tuft of hazel trees,
> That twinkle to the gusty breeze,
> Behold him perched in ecstacies,
>   Yet seeming still to hover,
> There! where the flutter of his wings
> Upon his back and body flings
> Shadows and sunny glimmerings
>   That cover him all over.
> While thus before my eyes he gleams,
> A brother of the leaves he seems:
> When in a moment forth he teems
>   His little song in gushes:
> As if it pleased him to disdain
> And mock the form which he did feign,
> While he was dancing with the train
>   Of leaves among the bushes.

Or the description of the blue-cap, and of the noontide silence or the poem to *The Cuckoo*, or, lastly, though I might multiply the references to ten times the number, to the poem so completely Wordsworth's commencing:

> Three years she grew in sun and shower.

Fifth: a meditative pathos, a union of deep and subtle thought with sensibility; a sympathy with man as man; the sympathy indeed of a contemplator, rather than a fellow-sufferer or comate (spectator, *haud particeps*), but of a contemplator, from whose view no difference of rank conceals the sameness of the nature; no injuries of wind or weather, of toil, or even of ignorance, wholly disguise the human face divine. The superscription and the image of the Creator still remain legible to him under the dark lines, with which guilt or calamity had cancelled or cross-barred it. Here the man and the poet lose and find themselves in each other, the one as glorified, the latter as substantiated. In this mild and philosophic pathos, Wordsworth appears to me without a compeer. Such he *is:* so he *writes.* "'Tis said that some have died for love,' or that most affecting composition, the *Affliction of Margaret —— of ——*, which no mother, and if I may judge by my own experience, no parent can read without a tear. Or turn to that genuine lyric, in the former edition, entitled, *The Mad Mother*, of which I cannot refrain from quoting two of the stanzas, both of them for their pathos, and the former for the fine transition in the two concluding lines of the stanza, so expressive of that deranged state, in which from the increased sensibility the sufferer's attention is abruptly drawn off by every trifle, and in the same instant plucked back again by the one despotic thought, and bringing home with it, by the blending, fusing power of Imagination and Passion, the alien object to which it had been so abruptly diverted, no longer an alien but an ally and an inmate:

> Suck, little babe, oh suck again!
> It cools my blood, it cools my brain:
> Thy lips, I feel them, baby! they
> Draw from my heart the pain away.
> Oh! press me with thy little hand;
> It loosens something at my chest;
> About that tight and deadly band
> I feel thy little fingers prest.
> The breeze I see is in the trees!
> It comes to cool my babe and me.
>
> Thy father cares not for my breast,
> 'Tis thine, sweet baby, there to rest.
> 'Tis all thine own! – and, if its hue

Be changed, that was so fair to view.
'Tis fair enough for thee, my dove!
My beauty, little child, is flown,
But thou wilt live with me in love,
And what if my poor cheek be brown
'Tis well for me, thou canst not see
How pale and wan it else would be.

Lastly, and pre-eminently, I challenge for this poet the gift of Imagination in the highest and strictest sense of the word. In the play of fancy, Wordsworth, to my feelings, is not always graceful, and sometimes recondite. The likeness is occasionally too strange, or demands too peculiar a point of view, or is such as appears the creature of predetermined research, rather than spontaneous presentation. Indeed his fancy seldom displays itself as mere and unmodified fancy. But in imaginative power, he stands nearest of all modern writers to Shakespeare and Milton; and yet in a king perfectly unborrowed and his own. To employ his own words, which are at once an instance and an illustration, he does indeed to all thoughts and to all objects:

> ...add the gleam,
> The light that never was on sea or land.
> The consecration, and the poet's dream.
> *Elegiac Stanzas on a Picture of Peele Castle.*

I shall select a few examples as most obviously manifesting this faculty; but if I should ever be fortunate enough to render my analysis of imagination, its origin and characters, thoroughly intelligible to the reader, he will scarcely open on a page of this poet's works without recognising, more or less, the presence and the influences of this faculty.

From the poem on *The Yew Trees:*

> But worthier still of note
> Are those fraternal four of Borrowdale,
> Joined in one solemn and capacious grove;
> Huge trunks! – and each particular trunk a growth
> Of intertwisted fibres serpentine
> Up-coiling, and inveterately convolved, –
> Not uninformed with phantasy, and looks

That threaten the profane; – a pillared shade,
Upon whose grassless floor of red-brown hue,
By sheddings from the pinal umbrage tinged
Perennially – beneath whose sable roof
Of boughs, as if for festal purpose decked
With unrejoicing berries, ghostly shapes
May meet at noontide – Fear and trembling Hope.
Silence and Foresight – Death, the skeleton,
And time, the shadow – there to celebrate,
As in a natural temple scattered o'er.
With altars undisturbed of mossy stone,
United worship; or in mute repose
To lie, and listen to the mountain flood
Murmuring from Glanamara's inmost caves.

The effect of the old man's figure in the poem of *Resolution and Independence*:

While he was talking thus, the lonely place,
The old man's shape, and speech, all troubled me;
In my mind's eye I seemed to see him pace
About the weary moors continually,
Wandering about alone and silently.

Or the 8th, 9th, 19th, 26th, 31st, and 33rd, in the collection of *Miscellaneous Sonnets* – the sonnet on the subjugation of Switzerland, or the last ode, from which I especially select the two following stanzas or paragraphs. (*On the Intimations of Immortality from Recollections of early Childhood:*

Our birth is but a sleep and a forgetting:
The soul that rises with us, our life's star
Hath had elsewhere its setting,
    And cometh from afar.
Not in entire forgetfulness,
And not in utter nakedness,
But trailing clouds of glory do we come
From God who is our home:
Heaven lies about us in our infancy!
Shades of the prison-house begin to close
    Upon the growing boy;
But he beholds the light, and whence it flows,

He sees it in his joy!
The youth who daily further from the east
Must travel, still is nature's priest,
 And by the vision splendid
 Is on his way attended;
At length the man perceives it die away,
And fade into the light of common day.

And from the same ode:

O joy that is our embers
Is something that doth live,
That nature yet remembers
What was so fugitive!
The thought of our past years in me doth breed
Perpetual benedictions: not indeed
For that which is most worthy to be blest;
Delight and liberty, the simple creed
Of childhood, whether busy or at rest,
With new-fledged hope still fluttering in his breast: –
Not for these I raise
The song of thanks and praise;
But for those obstinate questionings
Of sense and outward things,
Falling from us, vanishing;
Blank misgivings of a creature
Moving about in worlds not realised,
High instincts, before which our mortal nature
Did tremble like a guilty thing surprised!
But for those first affections,
Those shadowy recollections,
Which, be they what they may,
Are yet the fountain light of all our day,
Are yet a master light of all our seeing;
Upholds us – cherish – and have power to make
Our noisy years seem moments in the being
Of the eternal silence; truths that wake
To perish never:
Which neither listlessness, nor mad endeavour,
Nor man nor boy,
Nor all that is at enmity with joy
Can utterly abolish or destroy!

Hence, in a season of calm weather,
Though inland far we be,
Our souls have sight of that immortal sea
Which brought us hither,
Can in a moment travel thither –
And see the children sport upon the shore,
And hear the mighty waters rolling evermore.

And since it would be unfair to conclude with an extract, which though highly characteristic, must yet from the nature of the thoughts and the subjects be interesting, or perhaps intelligible, to but a limited number of readers; I will add from the poet's last published work a passage equally Wordsworthian; of the beauty of which, and of the imaginative power displayed therein, there can be but one opinion, and one feeling (See *The White Doe*):

Fast the church-yard fills; – anon
Look again and they are gone;
The cluster round the porch, and the folk
Who sate in the shade of the prior's oak!
And scarcely have they disappeared
Ere the prelusive hymn is heard:
With one consent the people rejoice,
Filling the church with a lofty voice!
They sing a service which they feel
For 'tis the sun-rise of their zeal
And faith and hope are in their prime
In great Eliza's golden time.

A moment ends the fervent din
And all is hushed without and within;
For though the priest more tranquilly
Recites the holy liturgy,
The only voice which you can hear
Is the river murmuring near.
When soft! – the dusky trees between
And down the path through the open green,
Where is no living thing to be seen;
And through yon gateway, where is found
Beneath the arch with ivy bound,
Free entrance to the church-yard ground;

And right across the verdant sod
Towards the very house of God;
Comes gliding in with lovely gleam,
Comes gliding in serene and slow,
Soft and silent as a dream,
A solitary doe!
White she is as lily of June,
And beauteous as the silver moon
When out of sight the clouds are driven
And she is left alone in heaven!·
Or like a ship some gentle day
In sunshine sailing far away –
A glittering ship that hath the plain
Of ocean for her own domain.

. . . . .

What harmonious pensive changes
Wait upon her as she ranges
Round and round this pile of state
Overthrown and desolate!
Now a step or two her way
Is through space of open day,
Where the enamoured sunny light
Brightens her that was so bright:
Now doth a delicate shadow fall,
Falls upon her like a breath
From some lofty arch or wall,
As she passes underneath.

The following analogy will, I am apprehensive, appear dim and
fantastic, but in reading Bartram's Travels I could not help
transcribing the following lines as a sort of allegory, or con-
nected simile and metaphor of Wordsworth's intellect and
genius. 'The soil is a deep, rich, dark mould, on a deep stratum
of tenacious clay; and that on a foundation of rocks, which often
break through both strata, lifting their backs above the surface.
The trees which chiefly grow here are the gigantic black oak;
magnolia grandiflora; fraximus excelsior; platane; and a few
stately tulip trees.' What Mr Wordsworth will produce, it is
not for me to prophesy: but I could pronounce with the liveliest
convictions what he is capable of producing. It is the FIRST
GENUINE PHILOSOPHIC POEM.

The preceding criticism will not, I am aware, avail to over-
come the prejudices of those who have made it a business to
attack and ridicule Mr Wordsworth's compositions.

Truth and prudence might be imaged as concentric circles.
The poet may perhaps have passed beyond the latter, but he has
confined himself far within the bounds of the former, in desig-
nating these critics, as too petulant to be passive to a genuine
poet, and too feeble to grapple with him: 'men of palsied
imaginations in whose minds all healthy action is languid; –
who therefore, feel as the many direct them, or with the many
are greedy after vicious provocatives.'

Let not Mr Wordsworth be charged with having expressed
himself too indignantly, till the wantonness and the systematic
and malignant perseverance of the aggressions have been taken
into fair consideration. I myself heard the commander-in-chief
of this unmanly warfare make a boast of his private admiration
of Wordsworth's genius. I have heard him declare, that whoever
came into his room would probably find the *Lyrical Ballads*
lying open on his table, and that (speaking exclusively of those
written by Mr Wordsworth himself) he could nearly repeat the
whole of them by heart. But a Review, in order to be a saleable
article, must be personal, sharp, and pointed: and, since then,
the poet has made himself, and with himself all who were, or
were supposed to be, his friends and admirers, the object of the
critic's revenge – how? by having spoken of a work so conducted
in the terms which it deserved! I once heard a clergyman in
boots and buckskin avow, that he would cheat his own father
in a horse. A moral system of a similar nature seems to have
been adopted by too many anonymous critics. As we used to say
at school, in reviewing they make believe being rogues: and
he who complains is to be laughed at for his ignorance of the
game. With the pen out of their hand they are honourable men.
They exert indeed power (which is to that of the injured party
who should attempt to expose their glaring perversions and
mis-statements, as twenty to one) to write down, and (where
the author's circumstances permit) to impoverish the man,
whose learning and genius they themselves in private have
repeatedly admitted. They knowingly strive to make it impos-
sible for the man even to publish any future work without

exposing himself to all the wretchedness of debt and embarrass-
ment. But this is all in their vocation: and bating what they do
in their vocation, 'who can say that black is the white of their
eye?'

So much for the detractors from Wordsworth's merits. On
the other hand, much as I might wish for their fuller sympathy,
I dare not flatter myself, that the freedom with which I have
declared my opinions concerning both his theory and his defects,
most of which are more or less connected with his theory either
as cause or effect, will be satisfactory or pleasing to all the poet's
admirers and advocates. More indiscriminate than mine their
admiration may be: deeper and more sincere it cannot be. But I
have advanced no opinion either for praise or censure, other
than as texts introductory to the reasons which compel me to
form it. Above all, I was fully convinced that such a criticism
was not only wanted; but that, if executed with adequate ability,
it must conduce in no mean degree to Mr Wordsworth's repu-
tation. His fame belongs to another age, and can neither be
accelerated nor retarded. How small the proportion of the
defects are to the beauties, I have repeatedly declared; and
that no one of them originates in deficiency of poetic genius.
Had they been more and greater, I should still, as a friend to
his literary character in the present age, consider an analytic
display of them as pure gain; if only it removed, as surely to all
reflecting minds even the foregoing analysis must have removed,
the strange mistake so slightly grounded, yet so widely and
industriously propagated, of Mr Wordsworth's turn for sim-
plicity! I am not half as much irritated by hearing his enemies
abuse him for vulgarity of style, subject, and conception, as I
am disgusted with the gilded side of the same meaning, as
displayed by some affected admirers with whom he is, forsooth,
'a sweet, simple poet!' and so natural, that little master Charles,
and his younger sister, are so charmed with them, that they play
at Goody Blake, or at Johnny and Betty Foy!

[*Biographia Literaria*]

KEATS

...WITH your patience, I will return to Wordsworth – whether or no he has an extended vision or a circumscribed grandeur – whether he is an eagle in his nest or on the wing; and, to be more explicit, and to show you how tall I stand by the giant, I will put down a simile of human life as far as I now perceive it; that is, to the point to which I say we both have arrived at. Well, I compare human life to a large mansion of many apartments, two of which I can only describe, the doors of the rest being as yet shut upon me. The first we step into we call the Infant, or Thoughtless Chamber, in which we remain as long as we do not think. We remain there a long while, and notwithstanding the doors of the second chamber remain wide open, showing a bright appearance we care not to hasten to it, but are at length imperceptibly impelled by the awakening of the thinking principle within us. We no sooner get into the second chamber, which I shall call the Chamber of Maiden-thought, than we become intoxicated with the light and the atmosphere. We see nothing but pleasant wonders, and think of delaying there for ever in delight. However, among the effects this breathing is father of, is that tremendous one of sharpening one's vision into the heart and nature of man, of convincing one's nerves that the world is full of misery and heartbreak, pain, sickness, and oppression; whereby this Chamber of Maiden-thought becomes gradually darkened, and at the same time, on all sides of it, many doors are set open – but all dark – all leading to dark passages. We see not the balance of good and evil; we are in a mist, *we* are in that state, we feel the 'Burden of the Mystery'. To this point was Wordsworth come, as far as I can conceive, when he wrote *Tintern Abbey*, and it seems to me that his genius is explorative of those dark passages. Now if we live, and go on thinking, we too shall explore them. He is a genius and superior [to] us, in so far as he can, more than we, make discoveries and shed a light in them. Here I must think it has depended more upon the general and gregarious advance of intellect than individual greatness of mind. From the *Paradise Lost*, and the other works of Milton, I hope it is not too presuming, even between ourselves, to say, that his philosophy, human and divine, may be tolerably understood by one not much advanced in years. In his time, Englishmen were just emancipated from a great superstition, and men had got hold of certain points and resting-places in reasoning which were too newly born to be doubted, and too much opposed by the rest of Europe, not to be thought ethereal and authentically divine. Who could gainsay his ideas on virtue, vice, and chastity, in *Comus*, just at the time of the dismissal of a hundred social disgraces? Who would not rest satisfied with his hintings at good and evil in the *Paradise Lost*, when just free from the Inquisition and burning in Smithfield? The Reformation produced such immediate and great benefits, that Protestantism was considered under the immediate eye of heaven, and its own remaining dogmas and superstitions then, as it were, regenerated, constituted those resting-places and seeming sure points of reasoning. From that I have mentioned, Milton, whatever he may have thought in the sequel, appears to have been content with these by his writings. He did not think with the human heart as Wordsworth has done; yet Milton, as a philosopher, had surely as great powers as Wordsworth. What is then to be inferred? O! many things: it proves there is really a grand march of intellect; it proves that a mighty Providence subdues the mightiest minds to the service of the time being, whether it be in human knowledge or religion.

[Life and Letters]

DE QUINCEY

ONE ORIGINAL obstacle to the favourable impression of the Wordsworthian poetry, and an obstacle purely self-created, was his theory of Poetic Diction. The diction itself, without the theory, was of less consequence; for the mass of readers would have been too blind or too careless to notice it. But the preface to the second edition of his poems (1799–1800 2 vols.) compelled all readers to notice it.

Nothing more injudicious was ever done by man. An unpopular truth would, at any rate, have been a bad inauguration for what, on *other* accounts, the author had announced as 'an experiment'. His poetry was already, and confessedly, an experiment as regarded the quality of the subjects selected, and as regarded the mode of treating them. That was surely trial enough for the reader's untrained sensibilities, without the unpopular novelty besides as to the quality of the diction. But, in the meantime, this novelty, besides being unpopular, was also in part false; it was true, and it was *not* true. And it was not true in a double way. Stating broadly, and allowing it to be taken for his meaning, that the diction of ordinary life (in his own words 'the very language of men') was the proper diction for poetry, the writer meant no such thing; for only a *part* of this diction, according to his own subsequent restriction, was available for such a use. And, secondly, as his own subsequent practice showed, even this part was available only for peculiar classes of poetry.

In his own exquisite *Laodamia*, in his *Sonnets*, in his *Excursion*, few are his obligations to the idiomatic language of life, as distinguished from that of books, or of prescriptive usage. Coleridge remarked justly, that *The Excursion* bristles beyond most poems with what are called 'dictionary' words, that is, polysyllabic words of Latin or Greek origin. And so it must ever be in meditative poetry upon solemn philosophic themes. The gamut of ideas needs a corresponding gamut of expressions; the scale of the thinking which ranges through *every* key exacts, for the artist, an unlimited command over the entire scale of the instrument which he employs. Never, in fact, was there a more erroneous direction – one falser in its grounds, or more ruinous in its tendency – than that given by a modern Rector of the Glasgow University to the students – *viz* that they should culti- vate the Saxon part of our language rather than the Latin part. Nonsense. Both are indispensable; and, speaking generally, without stopping to distinguish as to subjects, both are *equally* indispensable. Pathos, in situations which are homely, or at all connected with domestic affections, naturally moves by Saxon words. Lyrical emotion of every kind, which (to merit the name *lyrical*) must be in the state of flux and reflux, or, generally, of agitation, also requires the Saxon element of our language. And why? Because the Saxon is the aboriginal element, – the basis, and not the superstructure; consequently it comprehends all the ideas which are natural to the heart of man, and to the *elementary* situations of life. And, although the Latin often furnishes us with duplicates of these ideas, yet the Saxon, or monosyllabic part, has the advantage of precedency in our use and knowledge; for it is the language of the NURSERY, whether for rich or poor, – in which great philological academy no toleration is given to words in '*osity*' or '*ation*'. There is, therefore, a great advantage, as regards the consecration to our feelings, settled, by usage and custom, upon the Saxon strands in the mixed yarn of our native tongue. And, universally, this may be remarked – that wherever the passion of a poem is of that sort which *uses*, *presumes*, or *postulates* the ideas, without seeking to extend them, Saxon will be the 'cocoon' (to speak by the language applied to silkworms) which the poem spins for itself. But, on the other hand, where the motion of the feeling is *by* and *through* the ideas, where (as in religious or meditative poetry – Young's, for instance, or Cowper's) the sentiment creeps and kindles under- neath the very tissues of the thinking, there the Latin will predominate; and so much so that, whilst the flesh, the blood, and the muscle will be often almost exclusively Latin, the articulations or hinges of connexion and transition will be Anglo-Saxon.

But a blunder, more, perhaps from thoughtlessness and care- less reading than from malice, on the part of the professional

critics ought to have roused Wordsworth into a firmer feeling
of the entire question. These critics had fancied that, in Words-
worth's estimate, whatsoever was plebeian was also poetically
just in diction – not as though the impassioned phrase were
sometimes the vernacular phrase, but as though the vernacular
phrase were universally the impassioned. They naturally went
on to suggest, as a corollary which Wordsworth (as they
fancied) could not refuse, that Dryden and Pope must be trans-
lated into the flash diction of prisons and the slang of streets
before they could be regarded as poetically costumed. Now, so
far as these critics were concerned, the answer would have been
simply to say that much in the poets mentioned, but especially
of the racy Dryden, actually *is* in that vernacular diction for
which Wordsworth contended, and, for the other part, which is
not, frequently it *does* require the very purgation (if *that* were
possible) which the critics were presuming to be so absurd. In
Pope, and sometimes in Dryden, there is much of the unfeeling
and prescriptive diction which Wordsworth denounced. During
the eighty years between 1660 and 1740 grew up that scrofulous
taint in our diction which was denounced by Wordsworth as
technically received for 'poetic language'; and, if Dryden and
Pope were less infected than others, this was merely because
their understandings were finer. Much there is in both poets, as
regards diction, which *does* require correction, and correction of
the kind presumed by the Wordsworth theory. And, if, *so far*,
the critics should resist Wordsworth's principle of reform, not
he, but they, would have been found the patrons of deformity.
This course would soon have turned the tables upon the critics.
For the poets, or the class of poets, whom they unwisely selected
as models susceptible of no correction, happen to be those who
chiefly require it. But *their* foolish selection ought not to have
intercepted or clouded the true question when put in another
shape, since in this shape it opens into a very troublesome
dilemma. Spenser, Shakspere, the Bible of 1611, and Milton –
how say you, William Wordsworth – are these sound and true
as to diction, or are they not? If you say they *are*, then what is it
that you are proposing to change? What room for a revolution?
Would you, as Sancho says, have 'better bread than is made of
wheat'? But, if you say *No*, they are *not* sound, then, indeed, you

open a fearful range to your own artillery, but in a war greater than you could, by possibility, have contemplated.

In the first case, – that is, if the leading classics of the English literature are, in quality of diction and style, loyal to the canons of sound taste, – then you cut away the *locus standi* for yourself as a reformer: the reformation applies only to secondary and recent abuses. In the second case, if they also are faulty, you undertake an *onus* of hostility so vast that you will be found fighting against stars.

It is clear, therefore, that Wordsworth thus far erred, and caused needless embarrassment, equally to the attack and to the defence, by not assigning the names of the parties offending whom he had specially contemplated. The bodies of the criminals should have been had into court. But much more he erred in another point, where his neglect cannot be thought of without astonishment. The whole appeal turned upon a comparison between two modes of phraseology; each of which, the bad and the good, should have been extensively illustrated; and until that were done the whole dispute was an aerial subtlety, equally beyond the grasp of the best critic and the worst. How *could* a man so much in earnest, and so deeply interested in the question, commit so capital an oversight? *Tantamne rem tam negligenter?* (What! treat a matter so weighty in a style so slight and slip-shod?) The truth is that at this day, after a lapse of forty-seven years and much discussion, the whole question moved by Words-worth is still a *res integra* (a case untouched). And for this reason, – that no sufficient specimen has ever been given of the particular phraseology which each party contemplates as good or as bad; no man, in this dispute, steadily understands even himself; and, if he did, no other person understands him, for want of distinct illustrations. Not only the answer, therefore, is still entirely in arrear, but even the question is still in arrear: it has not yet practically explained itself so as that an answer to it could be possible.

. . . . . .

Not, therefore, in *The Excursion* must we look for that reversionary influence which awaits Wordsworth with posterity. It is the vulgar superstition in behalf of big books and sounding pretensions that must have prevailed upon Coleridge and others to undervalue, by comparison with the direct philosophic poetry of Wordsworth, those earlier poems which are all short, but generally scintillating with gems of far profounder truth. I speak of that truth which strengthens into solemnity an impression very feebly acknowledged previously, or truth which suddenly unveils a connexion between objects hitherto regarded as irrelate and independent. In astronomy, to gain the rank of discoverer, it is not required that you should reveal a star absolutely new: find out with respect to an old star some new affection – as, for instance, that it has an ascertainable parallax – and immediately you bring it within the verge of a human interest; or, with respect to some old familiar planet, that its satellites suffer periodical eclipses, and immediately you bring it within the verge of terrestial uses. Gleams of steadier vision that brighten into certainty appearances else doubtful, or that unfold relations else unsuspected, are not less discoveries of truth than the downright revelations of the telescope, or the absolute conquests of the diving-bell. It is astonishing how large a harvest of new truths would be reaped simply through the accident of a man's feeling or being made to feel, more *deeply* than other men. He sees the same objects, neither more nor fewer, but he sees them engraved in lines far stronger and more determinate: and the difference in the strength makes the whole difference between consciousness and subconsciousness. And in questions of the mere understanding we see the same fact illustrated. The author who wins notice the most is not he that perplexes men by truths drawn from fountains of absolute novelty, – truths as yet unsunned, and from that cause obscure, – but he that awakens into illuminated consciousness ancient lineaments of truth long slumbering in the mind, although too faint to have extorted attention. Wordsworth has brought many a truth into life, both for the eye and for the understanding, which previously had slumbered indistinctly for all men.

For instance, as respects the eye, who does not acknowledge instantaneously the magical strength of truth in his saying of a cataract seen from a station two miles off that it was 'frozen by distance'? In all nature there is not an object so essentially at war with the stiffening of frost as the headlong and desperate life of a cataract; and yet notoriously the effect of distance is to lock up this frenzy of motion into the most petrific column of stillness. This effect is perceived at once when pointed out; but how few are the eyes that ever *would* have perceived it for themselves! Twilight, again – who before Wordsworth ever distinctly noticed its *abstracting* power? – that power of removing, softening, harmonising, by which a mode of obscurity executes for the eye the same mysterious office which the mind so often, within its own shadowy realms, executes for itself. In the dim interspace between day and night all disappears from our earthly scenery, as if touched by an enchanter's rod, which is either mean or inharmonious, or unquiet, or expressive of temporary things. Leaning against a column of rock, looking down upon a lake or river, and at intervals carrying your eyes forward through a vista of mountains, you become aware that your sight rests upon the very same spectacle, unaltered in a single feature, which once at the same hour was beheld by the legionary Roman from his embattled camp, or by the roving Briton in his 'wolf-skin vest', lying down to sleep, and looking

> Through some leafy bower,
> Before his eyes were closed.

How magnificent is the summary or abstraction of the elementary features in such a scene, as executed by the poet himself, in illustration of this abstraction daily executed by Nature through her handmaid Twilight! Listen, reader, to the closing strain, solemn as twilight is solemn, and grand as the spectacle which it describes:

> By him (i.e. the roving Briton) was seen
> The self-same vision which *we* now behold,
> At thy meek bidding, shadowy Power, brought forth;
> These mighty barriers and the gulf between;
> The flood, the stars – a spectacle as old
> As the beginning of the heavens and earth.

Another great field there is amongst the pomps of nature which, if Wordsworth did not first notice, he certainly has noticed most circumstantially. I speak of cloud-scenery, or those pageants of sky-built architecture which sometimes in summer, at noon-

day, and in all seasons about sunset, arrest or appal the medita-
tive; 'perplexing monarchs' with the spectacle of armies
manœuvring, or deepening the solemnity of evening by towering
edifices that mimic – but which also in mimicking mock – the
transitory grandeurs of man. It is singular that these gorgeous
phenomena, not less than those of the *Aurora Borealis,* have been
so little noticed by poets. The *Aurora* was naturally neglected
by the southern poets of Greece and Rome, as not much seen in
their latitudes. But the cloud-architecture of the daylight belongs
alike to north and south. Accordingly, I remember one notice
of it in Hesiod, – a case where the clouds exhibited:

> The beauteous semblance of a flock at rest.

Another there is, a thousand years later, in Lucan: amongst the
portents which that poet notices as prefiguring the dreadful
convulsions destined to shake the earth at Pharsalia, I remember
some fiery coruscation of arms in the heavens; but, so far as I
recollect, the appearances might have belonged equally to the
workmanship of the clouds or the Aurora. Up and down the next
eight hundred years are scattered evanescent allusions to these
vapoury appearances; in *Hamlet* and elsewhere occur gleams of
such allusions; but I remember no distinct sketch of such an
appearance before that in the *Antony and Cleopatra* of Shakspere,
beginning:

> Sometimes we see a cloud that's dragonish.

Subsequently to Shakspere, these notices, as of all phenomena
whatsoever that demanded a familiarity with nature in the
spirit of love, became rarer and rarer. At length as the eighteenth
century was winding up its accounts, forth stepped William
Wordsworth; of whom, as a reader of all pages in nature, it may
be said that, if we except Dampier, the admirable buccaneer, the
gentle Filibuster, and some few professional naturalists, he first
and he last looked at natural objects with the eye that neither
will be dazzled from without nor cheated by preconceptions
from within. Most men look at nature in the hurry of a confusion
that distinguishes nothing; *their* error is from without. Pope,
again, and many who live in towns, make such blunders as that
of supposing the moon to tip with silver the hills *behind* which

[65]

she is rising, not by erroneous use of their eyes (for they use them not at all), but by inveterate preconceptions. Scarcely has there been a poet with what could be called a learned eye, or an eye *extensively* learned, before Wordsworth. Much affectation there has been of that sort since *his* rise, and at all times much counterfeit enthusiasm; but the sum of the matter is this, – that Wordsworth had his passion for nature fixed in his blood; it was a necessity, like that of the mulberry-leaf to the silk-worm; and through his commerce with nature did he live and breathe. Hence it was – *viz* from the *truth* of his love – that his knowledge grew; whilst most others, being merely hypocrites in their love, have turned our merely sciolists in their knowledge. This chapter, therefore, of *sky*-scenery may be said to have been revivified amongst the resources of poetry by Wordsworth – re-kindled, if not absolutely kindled. The sublime scene indorsed upon the draperies of the storm in the fourth book of the *Excursion* – that scene again witnessed upon the passage of the Hamilton Hills in Yorkshire – the solemn 'sky prospect' from the fields of France, – are unrivalled in that order of composition; and in one of these records Wordsworth has given first of all the true key-note of the sentiment belonging to these grand pageants. They are, says the poet, speaking in a case where the appearance had occurred towards night:

> Meek nature's evening comment on the shows
> And all the fuming vanities of earth.

Yes, that is the secret moral whispered to the mind. These mimicries express the laughter which is in heaven at earthly pomps. Frail and vapoury are the glories of man, even as the visionary parodies of those glories are frail, even as the scenical copies of those glories are frail, which nature weaves in clouds.

As another of those natural appearances which must have haunted men's eyes since the Flood, but yet had never forced itself into *conscious* notice until arrested by Wordsworth, I may notice an effect of *iteration* daily exhibited in the habits of cattle:

> The cattle are grazing
> Their heads never raising;
> There are forty feeding like one.

Now, merely as a *fact*, and if it were nothing more, this characteristic appearance in the habits of cows, when all repeat the action of each, ought not to have been overlooked by those who profess themselves engaged in holding up a mirror to nature. But the fact has also a profound meaning as a hieroglyphic. In all animals which live under the protection of man a life of peace and quietness, but do not share in his labours or in his pleasures, what we regard is the species, and not the individual. Nobody but a grazier ever looks at one cow amongst a field of cows, or at one sheep in a flock. But, as to those animals which are more closely connected with man, not passively connected, but actively, being partners in his toils, and perils, and recreations – such as horses, dogs, falcons – they are regarded as individuals, and are allowed the benefit of an individual interest. It is not that cows have not a differential character, each for herself; and sheep it is well known, have all a separate physiognomy for the shepherd who has cultivated their acquaintance. But men generally have no opportunity or motive for studying the individualities of creatures, however otherwise respectable, that are too much regarded by all of us in the reversionary light of milk, and beef, and mutton. Far otherwise it is with horses, who share in man's martial risks, who sympathise with man's frenzy in hunting, who divide with man the burdens of noonday. Far otherwise it is with dogs, that share the hearths of man, and adore the footsteps of his children. These man loves; of these he makes dear, though humble, friends. These often fight for *him;* and for *them* he reciprocally will sometimes fight. Of necessity, therefore, every horse and every dog is an individual – has a sort of personality that makes him *separately* interesting – has a beauty and a character of his own. Go to Melton, therefore, on some crimson morning, and what will you see? Every man, every horse, every dog, glorying in the plenitude of life is in a different attitude, motion, gesture, action. It is not there the sublime unity which you must seek, where forty are like one; but the sublime infinity; like that of ocean, like that of Flora, like that of nature, where no repetitions are endured, no leaf is the copy of another leaf, no absolute identity, and no painful tautologies. This subject might be pursued into profounder recesses; but in a popular discussion it is necessary to forbear.

A volume might be filled with such glimpses of novelty as Wordsworth has first laid bare, even to the apprehension of the *senses*. For the *understanding* when moving in the same track of human sensibilities, he has done only not so much. How often (to give an instance or two) must the human heart have felt the case, and yearned for an expression of the case, when there are sorrows which descend far below the region in which tears gather; and yet who has ever given utterance to this feeling until Wordsworth came with his immortal line:

Thoughts that do often lie too deep for tears?

This sentiment, and others that might be adduced (such as 'The child is father to the man'), have even passed into the popular heart, and are often quoted by those who know not *whom* they are quoting. Magnificent, again, is the sentiment, and yet an echo to one which lurks amongst all hearts, in relation to the frailty of merely human schemes for working good, which so often droop and collapse through the unsteadiness of human energies:

Foundations must be laid
In heaven.

How? Foundations laid in realms that are *above?* But *that* is impossible; *that* is at war with elementary physics; foundations must be laid *below*. Yes; and even so the poet throws the mind yet more forcibly on the hyperphysical character – on the grandeur transcending all physics – of those spiritual and shadowy foundations which alone are enduring.

But the great distinction of Wordsworth, and the pledge of his increasing popularity, is the extent of his sympathy with what is *really* permanent in human feelings, and also the depth of this sympathy. Young and Cowper, the two earlier leaders in the province of meditative poetry, are too circumscribed in the range of their sympathies, too narrow, too illiberal, and too exclusive. Both these poets manifested the quality of their strength in the quality of their public reception. Popular in some degree from the first, they entered upon the inheritance of their fame almost at once. Far different was the fate of Wordsworth:

for in poetry of this class, which appeals to what lies deepest in man, in proportion to the native power of the poet, and his fitness for permanent life, is the strength of resistance in the public taste. Whatever is too original will be hated at the first. It must slowly mould a public for itself; and the resistance of the early thoughtless judgments must be overcome by a counter-resistance to itself in a better audience slowly mustering against the first. Forty and seven years it is since William Wordsworth first appeared as an author. Twenty of those years he was the scoff of the world, and his poetry a byword of scorn. Since then and more than once, senates have rung with acclamations to the echo of his name. Now, at this moment, whilst we are talking about him, he has entered upon his seventy-sixth year. For himself, according to the course of nature, he cannot be far from his setting; but his poetry is only now clearing the clouds that gathered about its rising. Meditative poetry is perhaps that province of literature which will ultimately maintain most power amongst the generations which are coming; but in this department, at least, there is little competition to be apprehended by Wordsworth from anything that has appeared since the death of Shakspere.

[*On Wordsworth's Poetry*]

BAGEHOT

Now it came to pass in those days that William Wordsworth went up into the hills. It has been attempted in recent years to establish that the object of his life was to teach Anglicanism. A whole life of him has been written by an official gentleman, with the apparent view of establishing that the great poet was a believer in rood-lofts, an idolator of piscinae. But this is not capable of rational demonstration. Wordsworth, like Coleridge, began life as a heretic, and as the shrewd Pope unfallaciously said, 'once a heretic, always a heretic'. Sound men are sound from the first; safe men are safe from the beginning; and Wordsworth began wrong. His real reason for going to live in mountains was certainly in part sacred, but it was not in the least Tractarian:

> For he with many feelings, many thoughts,
> Made up a meditative joy, and found
> Religious meanings in the forms of nature.

His whole soul was absorbed in the one idea, the one feeling, the one thought of the sacredness of hills.

> Early had he learned
> To reverence the volume that displays
> The mystery, the life which cannot die:
> But in the mountains did he *feel* his faith
> All things responsive to the writing, there
> Breathed immortality, revolving life,
> And greatness still revolving; infinite;
> There littleness was not.
>   . . . . .
>
> A sense sublime
> Of something far more deeply interfused,
> Whose dwelling is the light of setting suns,
> And the round ocean and the living air
> And the blue sky, and in the mind of man.
> A motion and a spirit that impels
> All thinking things, all objects of all thought,
> And rolls through all things.

The defect of this religion is, that it is too abstract for the practical, and too bare for the musing. What active men require is personality; the meditative require beauty. But Wordsworth gave us neither. The worship of sensuous beauty – the southern religion – is of all sentiments the one most deficient in his writings. His poetry hardly even gives the charm, the entire charm, of the scenery in which he lived. The lighter parts are little noticed: the rugged parts protrude. The bare waste, the folding hill, the rough lake, Helvellyn with a brooding mist, Ulswater on a grey day, these are his subjects. He took a personal interest in the corners of the universe. There is a print of Rembrandt said to represent a piece of the Campagna, a mere waste, with a stump and a man, and under is written *'Tacet et loquitur'*, and thousands will pass the old print-shop where it hangs, and yet have a taste for paintings, and colours, and oils: but some fanciful students, some lonely stragglers, some long-haired enthusiasts, by chance will come, one by one, and look, and look, and be hardly able to take their eyes from the fascination, so massive is the shade, so still the conception, so firm the execution. Thus is it with Wordsworth and his poetry. *Tacet et loquitur.* Fashion apart, the million won't read it. Why should they? – they could not understand it, – don't put them out, – let them buy, and sell, and die, – but idle students, and enthusiastic wanderers, and solitary thinkers, will read, and read, and read, while their lives and their occupations hold. In truth, his works are the Scriptures of the intellectual life; for that same searching, and finding, and penetrating power which the real Scripture exercises on those engaged, as are the mass of men, in practical occupations and domestic ties, do his works exercise on the meditative, the solitary, and the young.

> His daily teachers had been woods and rills,
> The silence that is in the starry sky,
> The sleep that is among the lonely hills.

And he had more than others:

> That blessed mood,
> In which the burthen of the mystery,
> In which the heavy and the weary weight

Of all this unintelligible world
Is lightened: that serene and blessed mood
In which the affections gently lead us on,
Until the breath of this corporeal frame,
And even the motion of our human blood
Almost suspended, we are laid asleep
In body, and become a living soul;
While with an eye, made quiet by the power
Of harmony, and the deep power of joy,
We see into the life of things.

And therefore he has had a whole host of sacred imitators. Mr Keble, for example, has translated him for women. He has himself told us that he owed to Wordsworth the tendency *ad sanctiora*, which is the mark of his own writings; and in fact he has but adapted the tone and habit of reverence, which his master applied to common objects and the course of the seasons, to sacred objects and the course of the ecclesiastical year, – diffusing a mist of sentiment and devotion altogether delicious to a gentle and timid devotee. Hartley Coleridge is another translator. He has applied to the sensuous beauties and seductive parts of external nature the same *cultus* which Wordsworth applied to the bare and the abstract.

[Literary Studies]

CARLYLE

OF WORDSWORTH I have little to write that could ever be of use
to myself or others. I did not see him much, or till latish in my
course see him at all; nor did we deeply admire one another at
any time! Of me in my first times he had little knowledge; and
any feeling he had towards me, I suspect, was largely blended
with abhorrence and perhaps a kind of fear. His works I knew;
but never considerably reverenced, – could not, on attempting
it. A man recognisably of strong intellectual powers, strong
character; given to meditation and much contemptuous of the
*un*meditative world and its noisy nothingness; had a fine limpid
style of writing and delineating, in his small way; a fine limpid
vein of melody too in him (as of an honest rustic *fiddle*, good,
and well handled, but *wanting* two or more of the *strings*, and
not capable of much!) – in fact, a rather dull, hard-tempered,
unproductive and almost wearisome kind of man; not adorable,
by any means, as a great Poetic Genius, much less as the
Trismegistus of such; whom only a select few could even read,
instead of mis-reading, which was the opinion his worshippers
confidently entertained of him!

Privately I had a real respect for him withal, founded on his
early Biography, which Wilson of Edinburgh had painted to
me as of antique greatness signifying: 'Poverty and Peasanthood,
then; be it so. But we consecrate ourselves to the Muses, all the
same, and will proceed on those terms, Heaven aiding!' This, and
what of faculty I did recognise in the man, gave me a clear esteem
of him, as of one remarkable and fairly beyond common; – not to
disturb which, I avoided speaking of him to his worshippers; or,
if the topic turned up, would listen with an acquiescing air. But
to my private self his divine reflections and unfathomabilities
seemed stinted, scanty; palish and uncertain; – perhaps in part a
feeble *reflex* (derived at second hand through Coleridge) of the
immense German fund of such? – and I reckoned his Poetic Store-
house to be far from an opulent or well furnished apartment!

It was perhaps about 1840 that I first had any decisive meeting with Wordsworth, or made any really personal acquaintance with him. In parties at Taylor's I may have seen him before; but we had no speech together, nor did we specially notice one another: – one such time I do remember (probably *before*, as it was in my earlier days of Sterling acquaintanceship, when Sterling used to argue much with me), Wordsworth sat silent, almost next to me, while Sterling took to asserting the claims of Kotzebue as a Dramatist ('recommended even by Goethe', as he likewise urged); whom I with pleasure did my endeavour to explode from that mad notion, – and thought (as I still recollect), 'This will please Wordsworth too'; who, however, gave not the least sign of that or any other feeling. I had various dialogues with him in that same room; but these, I judge, were all or mostly of after date.

On a summer morning (let us call it 1840, then) I was apprised by Taylor that Wordsworth had come to Town; and would meet a small party of us at a certain Tavern in St James's Street, at breakfast, – to which I was invited for the given day and hour. We had a pretty little room; quiet, though looking street-ward (Tavern's *name* is quite lost to me); the morning sun was pleasantly tinting the opposite houses, a balmy, calm and bright morning: Wordsworth, I think, arrived just along with me; we had still five minutes of sauntering and miscellaneous talking before the whole were assembled. I do not positively remember any of them, except that James Spedding was there; and that the others, not above five or six in whole, were polite intelligent quiet persons, and, except Taylor and Wordsworth, not of any special distinction in the world. Breakfast was pleasant, fairly beyond the common of such things; Wordsworth seemed in good tone, and, much to Taylor's satisfaction, talked a great deal. About 'poetic' correspondents of his own (i.e. correspondents for the sake of *his* Poetry – especially, one such who had sent him, from Canton, an excellent *Chest of Tea*, correspondent grinningly applauded by us all); then about ruralities and miscellanies, 'Countess of Pembroke' (antique She – Clifford, glory of those Northern parts, who was not new to any of us, but was set forth by Wordsworth with gusto and brief emphasis, 'You lily-livered' etc) now the only memorable item under that head: these were the first topics. Then finally about *Literature*, literary laws, practices, observances, – at considerable length, and turning wholly on the mechanical part, including even a good deal of shallow enough *etymology*, from me and others, which was well received: on all this Wordsworth enlarged with evident satisfaction, and was joyfully reverent of the 'wells of English undefiled', – though stone *dumb* as to the deeper rules, and wells of Eternal Truth and Harmony you were to try and set forth by said undefiled wells of *English* or what other Speech you had! To me a little disappointing, but not much; – though it would have given me pleasure, had the robust veteran man emerged a little out of vocables into things, now and then, as he never once chanced to do. For the rest, he talked well in his way; with veracity, easy brevity and force; as a wise tradesman would of his tools and workshop, – and as no unwise one could. His voice was good, frank and sonorous, though practically clear, distinct and forcible, rather than melodious; the tone of him business-like, sedately confident, no discourtesy, yet no anxiety about being courteous; a fine wholesome rusticity, fresh as his mountain breezes, sat well on the stalwart veteran, and on all he said and did. You would have said he was a usually taciturn man; glad to unlock himself, to audience sympathetic and intelligent, when such offered itself. His face bore marks of much, not always peaceful, meditation; the look of it not bland or benevolent, so much as close, impregnable and hard: a man *multa tacere loquive paratus*, in a world where he had experienced no lack of contradictions as he strode along! The eyes were not very brilliant, but they had a quiet clearness; there was enough of brow, and well shaped; rather too much of cheek ('horse-face', I have heard satirists say), face of squarish shape and decidedly longish, as I think the head itself was (*its* 'length' going *horizontal*): he was a large-boned, lean, but still firm-knit, tall and strong-looking when he stood: a right good old steel-gray figure, with a fine rustic simplicity and dignity about him, and a veracious *strength* looking through him which might have suited one of those old steel-gray *Markgräfs* (Graf – Grau, 'Steel-gray') whom Henry the Fowler set up to ward the 'marches', and do battle with the intrusive Heathen, in a stalwart and judicious manner.

[*Reminiscences*]

JOHN STUART MILL

THIS STATE of my thoughts and feelings made the fact of my reading Wordsworth for the first time (in the autumn of 1828), an important event in my life. I took up the collection of his poems from curiosity, with no expectation of mental relief from it, though I had before resorted to poetry with that hope. In the worst period of my depression, I had read through the whole of Byron (then new to me), to try whether a poet, whose peculiar department was supposed to be that of the intenser feelings, could rouse any feeling in me. As might be expected, I got no good from this reading, but the reverse. The poet's state of mind was too like my own. His was the lament of a man who had worn out all pleasures, and who seemed to think that life, to all who possess the good things of it, must necessarily be the vapid, uninteresting thing which I found it. His Harold and Manfred had the same burden on them which I had; and I was not in a frame of mind to desire any comfort from the vehement sensual passion of his Giaours, or from the sullenness of his Laras. But while Byron was exactly what did not suit my condition, Wordsworth was exactly what did. I had looked into the *Excursion* two or three years before, and found little in it; and I should probably have found as little, had I read it at this time. But the miscellaneous poems, in the two-volume edition of 1815 (to which little of value was added in the latter part of the author's life), proved to be the precise thing for my mental wants at that particular juncture.

In the first place these poems addressed themselves power-fully to one of the strongest of my pleasurable susceptibilities, the love of rural objects and natural scenery; to which I had been indebted not only for much of the pleasure of my life, but quite recently for relief from one of my longest relapses into depression. In this power of rural beauty over me, there was a foundation laid for taking pleasure in Wordsworth's poetry; the more so, as his scenery lies mostly among mountains, which, owing to my early Pyrenean excursion, were my ideal of natural beauty. But Wordsworth would never have had any great effect on me, if he had merely placed before me beautiful pictures of natural scenery. Scott does this still better than Wordsworth, and a very second-rate landscape does it more effectually than any poet. What made Wordsworth's poems a medicine for my state of mind, was that they expressed, not mere outward beauty, but states of feeling, and of thought coloured by feeling, under the excitement of beauty. They seemed to be the very culture of the feelings, which I was in quest of. In them I seemed to draw from a source of inward joy, of sympathetic and imaginative pleasure, which could be shared in by all human beings; which had no connection with struggle or imperfection, but would be made richer by every improvement in the physical or social condition of mankind. From them I seemed to learn what would be the perennial sources of happiness, when all the greater evils of life shall have been removed. And I felt myself at once better and happier as I came under their influence. There have certainly been, even in our own age, greater poets than Wordsworth; but poetry of deeper and loftier feeling could not have done for me at that time what his did. I needed to be made to feel that there was real, permanent happiness in tranquil contemplation. Wordsworth taught me this not only without turning away from, but with a greatly increased interest in the common feelings and common destiny of human beings. And the delight which these poems gave me, proved that with culture of this sort, there was nothing to dread from the most confirmed habit of analysis. At the conclusion of the *Poems* came the famous Ode, falsely called Platonic, *Intimations of Immortality* in which, along with more than his usual sweetness of melody and rhythm, and along with the two passages of grand imagery but bad philosophy so often quoted, I found that he too had had similar experience to mine; that he also had felt that the first freshness of youthful enjoyment of life was not lasting; but that he had sought for compensation, and found it, in the way in which he was now teaching me to find it. The result was that I gradually, but completely, emerged from my habitual depression, and was never again subject to it. I long continued to value Wordsworth less according to his intrinsic merits, than by the measure of what he had done for me. Compared with the greatest poets, he may be said to be the poet of unpoetical natures, possessed of quiet and contemplative tastes. But unpoetical natures are precisely those which require poetic cultivation. This poetic cultivation Wordsworth is much more fitted to give, than poets who are intrinsically far more poets than he.

[Autobiography]

TAINE

Wordsworth, a new Cowper, with less talent and more ideas than the other, was essentially a man of inner feelings, that is, engrossed by the concerns of the soul. Such men ask what they have come to do in this world, and why life has been given to them; if they are right or wrong, and if the secret movements of their heart are conformable to the supreme law, without taking into account the visible causes of their conduct. Such, for men of this kind is the master conception which renders them serious, meditative, and as a rule gloomy.[1] They live with their eyes turned inwards, not to mark and classify their ideas, like physiologists, but as moralists to approve or blame their feelings. Thus understood, life becomes a grave business, of uncertain issue, on which we must incessantly and scrupulously reflect. Thus understood, the world changes its aspect; it is no longer a machine of wheels working into each other, as the philosopher says, nor a splendid blooming plant, as the artist feels, – it is the work of a moral being, displayed as a spectacle to moral beings.

Figure such a man facing life and the world; he sees them, and takes part in it, apparently like anyone else; but how different is he in reality! His great thought pursues him; and when he beholds a tree, it is to meditate on human destiny.

He finds or lends a sense to the least objects: a soldier marching to the sound of the drum makes him reflect on heroic sacrifice, the support of societies; a train of clouds lying heavily on the verge of a gloomy sky, endues him with that melancholy calm, so suited to nourish moral life. There is nothing which does not recall him to his duty and admonish him of his origin. Near or far, like a great mountain in a landscape, his philosophy will appear behind all his ideas and images. If he is restless, impassioned, sick with scruples, it will appear to him amidst storm and lightning, as it did to the genuine Puritans, to Cowper,

[1] The Jansenists, the Puritans and the Methodists are the extremes of this class.

Pascal, Carlyle. It will appear to him in a greyish kind of fog, imposing and calm, if he enjoys, like Wordsworth, a calm mind and a quiet life. Wordsworth was a wise and happy man, a thinker and a dreamer, who read and walked. He was from the first in tolerably easy circumstances, and had a small fortune. Happily married, amidst the favour of government and the respect of the public, he lived peacefully on the margin of a beautiful lake, in sight of noble mountains, in the pleasant retirement of an elegant house, amidst the admiration and attentions of distinguished and chosen friends, engrossed by contemplations which no storm came to distract, and by poetry which was produced without any hindrance. In this deep calm he listens to his own thoughts; the peace was so great, within him and around him, that he could perceive the imperceptible. 'To me, the meanest flower that blows, can give Thoughts that do often lie too deep for tears.' He saw a grandeur, a beauty, a teaching in the trivial events which weave the woof of our most commonplace days.

He needed not, for the sake of emotion, either splendid sights or unusual actions. The dazzling glare of lamps, the pomp of the theatre, would have shocked him; his eyes were too delicate, accustomed to quiet and uniform tints. He was a poet of the twilight. Moral existence in commonplace existence, such was his object – the object of his choice. His paintings are cameos with a grey ground, which have a meaning; designedly he suppresses all which might please the senses, in order to speak solely to the heart. Out of this character sprang a theory, – his theory of art, altogether spiritualistic, which, after repelling classical habits, ended by rallying Protestant sympathies, and won for him as many partisans as it had raised enemies. Since the only important thing is moral life, let us devote ourselves solely to nourishing it.

The reader must be moved, genuinely, with profit to his soul; the rest is indifferent: let us, then, show him objects moving in themselves, without dreaming of clothing them in a beautiful style. Let us strip ourselves of conventional language and poetic diction. Let us neglect noble words, scholastic and courtly epithets, and all the pomp of factitious splendour, which the classical writers thought themselves bound to assume, and justified in imposing. In poetry, as elsewhere, the grand question is, not ornament, but truth. Let us leave show, and seek effect. Let us speak in a bare style, as like as possible to prose, to ordinary conversation, even to rustic conversation, and let us choose our subjects at hand, in humble life. Let us take for our characters an idiot boy, a shivering old peasant woman, a hawker, a servant stopping in the street. It is the truth of sentiment, not the dignity of the folks, which makes the beauty of a subject; it is the truth of sentiment, not the dignity of the words, which makes the beauty of poetry. What matters that it is a villager who weeps, if these tears enable me to see the maternal sentiment? What matters that my verse is a line of rhymed prose, if this line displays a noble emotion? Men read that they may carry away emotion, not phrases; they come to us to look for moral culture, not pretty ways of speaking. And thereupon Wordsworth, classifying his poems according to the different faculties of men and the different ages of life, undertakes to lead us through all compartments and degrees of inner education, to the convictions and sentiments which he has himself attained.

All this is very well, but on condition that the reader is in Wordsworth's position; that is, essentially a philosophical moralist, and an excessively sensitive man. When I shall have emptied my head of all worldly thoughts, and looked up at the clouds for ten years to refine my soul, I shall love this poetry. Meanwhile the web of imperceptible threads by which Wordsworth endeavours to bind together all sentiments and embrace all nature, breaks in my fingers; it is too fragile; it is a woof of woven spider-web, spun by a metaphysical imagination, and tearing as soon as a hand of flesh and blood tries to touch it.

[*History of English Literature*]

PATER

AN INTIMATE consciousness of the expression of natural things, which weighs, listens, penetrates, where the earlier mind passed roughly by, is a large element in the complexion of modern poetry. It has been marked as a fact in mental history again and again. It reveals itself in many forms; but is strongest and most ·attractive in what is strongest and most attractive in modern literature. It is exemplified, almost equally, by writers as unlike each other as Senacour and Théophile Gautier: as a singular chapter in the history of the human mind, its growth might be traced from Rousseau to Chateaubriand, from Chateaubriand to Victor Hugo: it has doubtless some latent connexion with those pantheistic theories which locate an intelligent soul in material things, and have largely exercised men's minds in some modern systems of philosophy: it is traceable even in the graver writings of historians: it makes as much difference between ancient and modern landscape art, as there is between the rough masks of an early mosaic and a portrait by Reynolds or Gainsborough. Of this new sense, the writings of Wordsworth are the central and elementary expression: he is more simply and entirely occupied with it than any other poet, though there are fine expressions of precisely the same thing in so different a poet as Shelley. There was in his own character a certain contentment, a sort of inborn religious placidity, seldom found united with a sensibility so mobile as his, which was favourable to the quiet, habitual observation of inanimate, or imperfectly animate, existence. His life of eighty years is divided by no very profoundly felt incidents: its changes are almost wholly inward, and it falls into broad, untroubled, perhaps somewhat monotonous spaces. What it most resembles is the life of one of those early Italian or Flemish painters, who, just because their minds were full of heavenly visions, passed, some of them, the better part of sixty years in quiet, systematic industry. This placid life matured a quite unusual sensibility, really innate in him, to the sights and sounds of the natural world – the flower and its shadow on the stone, the cuckoo and its echo. The poem of *Resolution and Independence* is a storehouse of such records: for its fulness of imagery it may be compared to Keats's *Saint Agnes' Eve*. To read one of his longer pastoral poems for the first time, is like a day spent in a new country: the memory is crowded for a while with its precise and vivid incidents:

> The pliant harebell swinging in the breeze
> On some grey rock –
>
> The single sheep and the one blasted tree
> And the bleak music from that old stone wall –
>
> In the meadows and the lower ground
> Was all the sweetness of a common dawn –
>
> And the green corn all day is rustling in thine ears.

Clear and delicate at once, as he is in the outlining of visible imagery, he is more clear and delicate still, and finely scrupulous, in the noting of sounds; so that he conceives of noble sound as even moulding the human countenance to nobler types, and as something actually 'profaned' by colour, by visible form, or image. He has a power likewise of realising, and conveying to the consciousness of the reader, abstract and elementary impressions – silence, darkness, absolute motionlessness: or, again, the whole complex sentiment of a particular place, the abstract expression of desolation in the long white road, of peacefulness in a particular folding of the hills. In the airy building of the brain, a special day or hour even, comes to have for him a sort of personal identity, a spirit or angel given to it, by which, for its exceptional insight, or the happy light upon it, it has a presence in one's history, and acts there, as a separate power or accomplishment; and he has celebrated in many of his poems the 'efficacious spirit', which, as he says, resides in these 'particular spots' of time.

It is to such a world, and to a world of congruous meditation thereon, that we see him retiring in his but lately published poem of *The Recluse* – taking leave, without much count of costs, of the world of business, of action and ambition, as also of all that for the majority of mankind counts as sensuous enjoyment.

And so it came about that this sense of a life in natural objects, which in most poetry is but a rhetorical artifice, is with Wordsworth the assertion of what for him is almost literal fact. To him every natural object seemed to possess more or less of a moral or spiritual life, to be capable of a companionship with man, full of expression, of inexplicable affinities and delicacies of intercourse. An emanation, a particular spirit, belonged, not to the moving leaves or water only, but to the distant peak of the hills arising suddenly, by some change of perspective, above the nearer horizon, to the passing space of light across the plain, to the lichened Druidic stone even, for a certain weird fellowship in it with the moods of men. It was like a 'survival', in the peculiar intellectual temperament of a man of letters at the end of the eighteenth century, of that primitive condition, which some philosophers have traced in the general history of human culture, wherein all outward objects alike, including even the works of men's hands, were believed to be endowed with animation, and the world was 'full of souls' – that mood in which the old Greek gods were first begotten, and which had many strange aftergrowths.

In the early ages, this belief, delightful as its effects on poetry often are, was but the result of a crude intelligence. But, in Wordsworth, such power of seeing life, such perception of a soul, in inanimate things, came to an exceptional susceptibility to the impressions of eye and ear, and was, in its essence, a kind of sensuousness. At least, it is only in a temperament exceptionally susceptible on the sensuous side, that this sense of the expressiveness of outward things comes to be so large a part of life. That he awakened 'a sort of thought in sense', is Shelley's just estimate of this element in Wordsworth's poetry.

And it was through nature, thus ennobled by a semblance of passion and thought, that he approached the spectacle of human life. Human life, indeed, is for him, at first, only an additional, accidental grace on the expressive landscape. When he thought of man, it was of man as in the presence and under the influence of these effective natural objects, and linked to them by many associations. The close connection of man with natural objects, the habitual association of his thoughts and feelings with a particular spot of earth, has sometimes seemed to degrade those who are subject to its influence, as if it did but reinforce that physical connexion of our nature with the actual lime and clay of the soil, which is always drawing us nearer to our end. But for Wordsworth, these influences tended to the dignity of human nature, because they tended to tranquillise it. By raising nature to the level of human thought he gives it power and expression: he subdues man to the level of nature, and gives him thereby a certain breadth and coolness and solemnity. The leech-gatherer on the moor, the woman 'stepping westward' are for him natural objects, almost in the same sense as the aged thorn, or the lichened rock on the heath. In this sense the leader of the 'Lake School' in spite of an earnest preoccupation with man, his thoughts, his destiny, is the poet of nature. And of nature, after all, in its modesty. The English lake country has, of course, its grandeurs. But the peculiar function of Wordsworth's genius, as carrying in it a power to open out the soul of apparently little or familiar things, would have found its true test had he become the poet of Surrey, say! and the prophet of its life. The glories of Italy and Switzerland, though he did write a little about them, had too potent a material life of their own to serve greatly his poetic purpose.

Religious sentiment, consecrating the affections and natural regrets of the human heart, above all, that pitiful awe and care for the perishing human clay, of which relic-worship is but the corruption, has always had much to do with localities, with the thoughts which attach themselves to actual scenes and places. Now what is true of it everywhere, is truest of it in those secluded valleys where one generation after another maintains the same abiding-place; and it was on this side, that Wordsworth apprehended religion most strongly. Consisting, as it did so much, in the recognition of local sanctities, in the habit of connecting the stones and trees of a particular spot of earth with the great events of life, till the low walls, the green mounds, the half-obliterated epitaphs seemed full of voices, and a sort of natural oracles, the very religion of these people of the dales appeared but as another link between them and the earth, and was literally a religion of nature. It tranquillised them by bringing them under the placid rule of traditional and narrowly localised observances. 'Grave livers', they seemed to him, under this aspect, with stately speech, and something of that natural dignity of manners, which underlies the highest courtesy.

And, seeing man thus as a part of nature, elevated and solemnised in proportion as his daily life and occupations brought him into companionship with permanent natural objects, his very religion forming new links for him with the narrow limits of the valley, the low vaults of his church, the rough stones of his home, made intense for him now with profound sentiment. Wordsworth was able to appreciate passion in the lowly. He chooses to depict people from humble life, because, being nearer to nature than others, they are on the whole more impassioned, certainly more direct in their expression of passion than other men; it is for this direct expression of passion that he values their humble words. In much that he said in exaltation of rural life, he was but pleading indirectly for that sincerity, that perfect fidelity to one's own inward presentations, to the precise features of the picture within, without which any profound poetry is impossible. It was not for their tameness, but for this passionate sincerity, that he chose incidents and situations from common life, 'related in a selection of language really used by men'. He constantly endeavours to bring his language near to the real language of men: to the real language of men, however, not on the dead level of their ordinary intercourse, but in select moment of vivid sensation, when this language is winnowed and ennobled by excitement. There are poets who have chosen rural life as their subject, for the sake of its passionless repose, and times when Wordsworth himself extols the mere calm and dispassionate survey of things as the highest aim of poetical culture. But it was not for such passionless calm that he preferred the scenes of pastoral life; and the meditative poet, sheltering himself, as it might seem, from the agitations of the outward world, is in reality only clearing the scene for the great exhibitions of emotion, and what he values most is the almost elementary expression of elementary feelings.

And so he has much for those who value highly the concentrated presentment of passion, who appraise men and women by their susceptibility to it, and art and poetry as they afford the spectacle of it. Breaking from time to time into the pensive spectacle of their daily toil, their occupations near to nature, come those great elementary feelings, lifting and solemnising their language and giving it a natural music. The great, distinguishing passion came to Michael by the sheepfold, to Ruth by the wayside, adding these humble children of the furrow to the true aristocracy of passionate souls. In this respect, Wordsworth's work resembles most that of George Sand, in those of her novels which depict country life. With a penetrative pathos, which puts him in the same rank with the masters of the sentiment of pity in literature, with Meinhold and Victor Hugo, he collects all the traces of vivid excitement which were to be found in that pastoral world – the girl who rung her father's knell; the unborn infant feeling about its mother's heart; the instinctive touches of children; the sorrows of the wild creatures, even – their home-sickness, their strange yearnings, the tales of passionate regret that hang by a ruined farm-building, a heap of stones, a deserted sheepfold; that gay, false, adventurous, outer world, which breaks in from time to time to bewilder and deflower these quiet homes; not 'passionate sorrow' only, for the overthrow of the soul's beauty, but the loss of, or carelessness for personal beauty even, in those whom men have wronged – their pathetic wanness; the sailor 'who, in his heart, was half a shepherd on the stormy seas'; the wild woman teaching her child to pray for her betrayer; incidents like the making of the shepherd's staff, or that of the young boy laying the first stone of the sheepfold; – all the pathetic episodes of their humble existence, their longing, their wonder at fortune, their poor pathetic pleasures, like the pleasures of children, won so hardly in the struggle for bare existence; their yearning towards each other, in their darkened houses, or at their early toil. A sort of biblical depth and solemnity hangs over this strange, new, passionate, pastoral world, of which he first raised the image, and the reflection of which some of our best modern fiction has caught from him.

He pondered much over the philosophy of his poetry, and reading deeply in the history of his own mind, seems at times to have passed the borders of a world of strange speculations, inconsistent enough, had he cared to note such inconsistencies, with those traditional beliefs, which were otherwise the object of his devout acceptance. Thinking of the high value he set upon customariness, upon all that is habitual, local, rooted in the ground, in matters of religious sentiment, you might sometimes regard him as one tethered down to a world, refined and peaceful indeed, but with no broad outlook, a world protected, but somewhat narrowed, by the influence of received ideas. But he is at times also something very different from this, and something much bolder. A chance expression is overheard and placed in a new connexion, the sudden memory of a thing long past occurs to him, a distant object is relieved for a while by a random gleam of light – accidents turning up for a moment what lies below the surface of our immediate experience – and he passes from the humble graves and lowly arches of 'the little rock-like pile' of a Westmoreland church, on bold trains of speculative thought, and comes, from point to point, into strange contact with thoughts which have visited, from time to time, far more venturesome, perhaps errant, spirits. He had pondered deeply, for instance, on those strange reminiscences and forebodings, which seem to make our lives stretch before and behind us, beyond where we can see or touch anything, or trace the lines of connection. Following the soul, backwards and forwards, on these endless ways, his sense of man's dim, potential powers became a pledge to him, indeed, of a future life, but carried him back also to that mysterious notion of an earlier state of existence – the fancy of the Platonists – the old heresy of Origen. It was in this mood that he conceived those oft reiterated regrets for a half-ideal childhood, when the relics of Paradise still clung about the soul – a childhood, as it seemed, full of the fruits of old age, lost for all, in a degree, in the passing away of the youth of the world, lost for each one, over again, in the passing away of actual youth. It is this ideal childhood which he celebrates in his famous *Ode on the Recollections of Childhood*, and some other poems which may be grouped around it, such as the lines on *Tintern Abbey*, and something like what he describes was actually truer of himself than he seems to have understood; for his own most delightful poems were really the instinctive productions of earlier life, and most surely for him, 'the first diviner influence of this world' passed away, more and more completely, in his contact with experience.

Sometimes as he dwelt upon those moments of profound, imaginative power, in which the outward objects appear to take colour and expression, a new nature almost, from the prompting of the observant mind, the actual world would, as it were, dissolve and detach itself, flake by flake, and he himself seemed to be the creator, and then he would be the destroyer, of the world in which he lived – that old isolating thought of many a brain-sick mystic of ancient and modern times. At other times, again, in those periods of intense susceptibility, in which he appeared to himself as but the passive recipient of external influences, he was attracted by the thought of a spirit of life in outward things, a single all-pervading mind in them, of which man, and even the poet's imaginative energy, are but moments – that old dream of the *anima mundi*, the mother of all things and their grave, in which some had desired to lose themselves, and others had become indifferent to the distinctions of good and evil. It would come, sometimes, like the sign of the *macrocosm* to Faust in his Cell: the network of man and nature was seen to be pervaded by a common, universal life: a new, bold thought lifted him above the furrow, above the green turf of the Westmoreland churchyard, to a world altogether different in its vagueness and vastness, and the narrow glen was full of the brooding power of one universal spirit.

And so he has something, also, for those who feel the fascination of bold speculative ideas, who are really capable of rising upon them to conditions of poetical thought. He uses them, indeed, always with a very fine apprehension of the limits within which alone philosophical imaginings have any place in true poetry; and using them only for poetical purposes, is not too careful even to make them consistent with each other. To him, theories which for other men bring a world of technical diction, brought perfect form and expression, as in those two lofty books of *The Prelude*, which describe the decay and the restoration of Imagination and Taste. Skirting the borders of this world of bewildering heights and depths, he got but the first exciting influence of it, that joyful enthusiasm which great imaginative theories prompt, when the mind first comes to have an understanding of them; and it is not under the influence of these thoughts that his poetry becomes tedious or loses its blitheness. He keeps them, too, always within certain ethical bounds, so that no word of his could offend the simplest of those simple souls which are always the largest portion of mankind. But it is, nevertheless, the contact of these thoughts, the speculative boldness in them, which constitutes, at least for some minds, the secret attraction of much of his best poetry – the sudden passage from lowly thoughts and places to the majestic forms of philosophical imagination, the play of these forms over a world so different, enlarging so strangely the bounds of its humble churchyards, and breaking such a wild light on the graves of christened children.

And these moods always brought with them faultless expression. In regard to expression, as with feeling and thought, the duality of the higher and lower moods was absolute. It belonged to the higher, the imaginative mood, and was the pledge of its reality, to bring the appropriate language with it. In him, when the really poetical motive worked at all, it united, with absolute justice, the word and the idea; each, in the imaginative flame, becoming inseparably one with the other, by that fusion of matter and form, which is the characteristic of the highest poetical expression. His words are themselves thought and feeling; not eloquent, or musical words merely, but that sort of creative language which carries the reality of what it depicts, directly to the consciousness.

The music of mere metre performs but a limited, yet a very peculiar and subtly ascertained function, in Wordsworth's poetry. With him, metre is but an additional grace, accessory to that deeper music of words and sounds, that moving power, which they exercise in the nobler prose no less than in formal poetry. It is a sedative to that excitement, an excitement sometimes almost painful, under which the language, alike of poetry and prose, attains a rhythmical power, independent of metrical combination, and dependent rather on some subtle adjustment of the elementary sounds of words themselves to the image of feeling they convey. Yet some of his pieces, pieces prompted by a sort of half-playful mysticism, like the *Daffodils* and *The Two April Mornings*, are distinguished by a certain quaint gaiety of metre, and rival by their perfect execution, in this respect, similar pieces among our own Elizabethan, or contemporary French poetry. And those who take up these poems after an interval of months, or years perhaps, may be surprised at finding how well old favourites wear, how their strange inventive turns of diction or thought still send through them the old feeling of surprise. Those who lived about Wordsworth were all great lovers of the older English literature, and oftentimes there came out in him a noticeable likeness to our earlier poets. He quotes unconsciously, but with new power of meaning, a clause from one of Shakespeare's sonnets; and as with some other men's most famous work, the *Ode on the Recollections of Childhood* had its anticipator.[2] He drew something too from the unconscious mysticism of the old English language itself, drawing out the inward significance of its racy idiom, and the not wholly unconscious poetry of the language used by the simplest people under strong excitement – language, therefore, at its origin.

The office of the poet is not that of the moralist, and the first aim of Wordsworth's poetry is to give the reader a peculiar kind of pleasure. But through his poetry, and through this pleasure in it, he does actually convey to the reader an extraordinary wisdom in the things of practice. One lesson, if men must have lessons, he conveys more clearly than all, the supreme importance of contemplation in the conduct of life. Contemplation – impassioned contemplation – that, is with Wordsworth the end-in-itself, the perfect end. We see the majority of mankind going most often to definite ends, lower or higher ends, as their own instincts may determine; but the end may never be attained, and the means not be quite the right means, great ends and little ones alike being, for the most part, distant, and the ways to them, in this dim world, somewhat vague. Meantime, to higher or lower ends, they move too often with something of a sad countenance, with hurried and ignoble gait, becoming, unconsciously, something like thorns, in their anxiety to bear grapes; it being possible for people, in the pursuit of even great ends, to become themselves thin and impoverished in spirit and temper, thus diminishing the sum of perfection in the world, at its very sources. We understand this when it is a question o

2 Henry Vaughan, in *The Retreat*.

mean, or of intensely selfish ends – of Grandet, or Javert. We think it bad morality to say that the end justifies the means, and we know how false to all higher conceptions of the religious life is the type of one who is ready to do evil that good may come. We contrast with such dark, mistaken eagerness, a type like that of Saint Catherine of Sienna, who made the means to her ends so attractive, that she won for herself an undying place in the *House Beautiful*, not by her rectitude of soul only, but by its 'fairness' – by those quite different qualities which commend themselves to the poet and the artist.

Yet, for most of us, the conception of means and ends covers the whole of life, and is the exclusive type or figure under which we represent our lives to ourselves. Such a figure, reducing all things to machinery, though it has on its side the authority of that old Greek moralist who has fixed for succeeding generations the outline of the theory of right living, is too like a mere picture or description of men's lives as we actually find them, to be the basis of the higher ethics. It covers the meanness of men's daily lives, and much of the dexterity and the vigour with which they pursue what may seem to them the good of themselves or of others; but not the intangible perfection of those whose ideal is rather in *being* than in *doing* – not those *manners* which are, in the deepest as in the simplest sense, *morals*, and without which one cannot so much as offer a cup of water to a poor man without offence – not the part of 'antique Rachel', sitting in the company of Beatrice; and even the moralist might well endeavour rather to withdraw men from the too exclusive consideration of means and ends, in life.

Against this predominance of machinery in our existence, Wordsworth's poetry, like all great art and poetry, is a continual protest. Justify rather the end by the means, it seems to say: whatever may become of the fruit, make sure of the flowers and the leaves. It was justly said, therefore, by one who had meditated very profoundly on the true relation of means to ends in life, and on the distinction between what is desirable in itself and what is desirable only as machinery, that when the battle which he and his friends were waging had been won, the world would need more than ever those qualities which Wordsworth was keeping alive and nourishing.

That the end of life is not action but contemplation – *being* as distinct from *doing* – a certain disposition of the mind: is, in some shape or other, the principle of all the higher morality. In poetry, in art, if you enter into their true spirit at all, you touch this principle, in a measure: these, by their very sterility, are a type of beholding for the mere joy of beholding. To treat life in the spirit of art, is to make life a thing in which means and ends are identified: to encourage such treatment, the true moral significance of art and poetry. Wordsworth, and other poets who have been like him in ancient or more recent times, are the masters, the experts, in this art of impassioned contemplation. Their work is, not to teach lessons, or enforce rules, or even to stimulate us to noble ends; but to withdraw the thoughts for a little while from the mere machinery of life, to fix them, with appropriate emotions on the spectacle of those great facts in man's existence which no machinery affects, 'on the great and universal passions of men, the most general and interesting of their occupations, and the entire world of nature', – on 'the operations of the elements and the appearance of the visible universe, on storm and sunshine, on the revolutions of the seasons on cold and heat, on the loss of friends and kindred, on injuries and resentments, on gratitude and hope, on fear and sorrow'.

To witness this spectacle with appropriate emotions is the aim of all culture; and of these emotions poetry like Wordsworth's is a great nourisher and stimulant. He sees nature full of sentiment and excitement; he sees men and women as parts of nature, passionate, excited, in strange grouping and connection with the grandeur and beauty of the natural world: – images, in his own words, 'of man suffering, amid awful forms and powers'.

Such is the figure of the more powerful and original poet, hidden away, in part under those weaker elements in Wordsworth's poetry, which for some minds determine their entire character; a poet somewhat bolder and more passionate than might at first be supposed, but not too bold for true poetical taste; an unimpassioned writer, you might sometimes fancy, yet thinking the chief aim, in life and art alike, to be a certain deep emotion; seeking most often the great elementary passions in lowly places; having at least this condition of all impassioned work, that he aims always at an absolute sincerity of feeling and diction, so that he is the true forerunner of the deepest and most passionate poetry of our own day, yet going back also, with something of a protest against the conventional fervour of much of the poetry popular in his own time, to those older English poets, whose unconscious likeness often comes out in him.

[Appreciations]

ARNOLD

To EXHIBIT this body of Wordsworth's best work, to clear away obstructions from around it, and to let it speak for itself, is what every lover of Wordsworth should desire. Until this has been done, Wordsworth, whom we, to whom he is dear, all of us know and feel to be so great a poet, has not had a fair chance before the world. When once it has been done, he will make his way best, not by our advocacy of him, but by his own worth and power. We may safely leave him to make his way thus, we who believe that a superior worth and power in poetry finds in mankind a sense responsive to it and disposed at last to recognise it. Yet at the outset, before he has been duly known and recognised, we may do Wordsworth a service, perhaps by indicating in what his superior power and worth will be found to consist, and in what it will not.

Long ago, in speaking of Homer, I said that the noble and profound application of ideas to life, is the most essential part of poetic greatness, – I said that an application of these ideas under the conditions fixed for us by the laws of poetic beauty and poetic truth. If it is said that to call these ideas *moral* ideas is to introduce a strong and injurious limitation, I answer that it is to do nothing of the kind, because moral ideas are really so main a part of human life. The question, *how to live*, is itself a moral idea; and it is the question which most interests every man, and with which, in some way or other, he is perpetually occupied. A large sense is of course to be given to the term *moral*. Whatever bears upon the question, 'how to live', comes under it:

> Nor love thy life, nor hate but, what thou liv'st,
> Live well; how long or short, permit to heaven.

In those fine lines Milton utters, as every one at once perceives, a moral idea. Yes, but so too, when Keats consoles the forward-bending lover on the Grecian Urn, the lover arrested and presented in immortal relief by the sculptor's hand before he can kiss, with the line:

For ever wilt thou love, and she be fair –

he utters a moral idea. When Shakespeare says that:

> We are such stuff
> As dreams are made on, and our little life
> Is rounded with a sleep –

he utters a moral idea.

Voltaire was right in thinking that the energetic and profound treatment of moral ideas, in this large sense, is what distinguishes the English poetry. He sincerely meant praise, not dispraise or hint of limitation; and they err who suppose that poetic limitation is a necessary consequence of the fact, the fact being granted as Voltaire states it. If what distinguishes the greatest poets is their powerful and profound application of ideas to life, which surely no good critic will deny, then to prefix to the term ideas here the term moral makes hardly any difference, because human life itself is in so preponderating a degree moral.

It is important, therefore, to hold fast to this: that poetry is at bottom a criticism of life; that the greatness of a poet lies in his powerful and beautiful application of ideas to life, – to the question: How to live? Morals are often treated in a narrow and false fashion; they are bound up with systems of thought and belief which have had their day; they are fallen into the hands of pedants and professional dealers; they grow tiresome to some of us. We find attraction, at times, even in a poetry of revolt against them; in a poetry which might take for its motto Omar Khayyam's words: 'Let us make up in the tavern for the time which we have wasted in the mosque.' Or we find attractions in a poetry indifferent to them; in a poetry where the contents may be what they will, but where the form is studied and exquisite. We delude ourselves in either case; and the best cure for our delusion is to let our minds rest upon that great and inexhaustible word *life*, until we learn to enter into its meaning. A poetry of revolt against moral ideas is a poetry of revolt against *life*; a poetry of indifference towards moral ideas is a poetry of indifference towards *life*.

Epictetus had a happy figure for things like the play of the senses, or literary form and finish, or argumentative ingenuity, in comparison with 'the best and master thing' for us, as he called it, the concern, how to live. Some people were afraid of them, he said, or they disliked and undervalued them. Such people were wrong; they were unthankful or cowardly. But the things might also be over-prized, and treated as final when they are not. They bear to life the relation which inns bear to home. 'As if a man, journeying home, and finding a nice inn on the road, and liking it, were to stay for ever at the inn! Man, thou hast forgotten thine object; thy journey was not *to* this, but *through* this. 'But this inn is taking.' And how many other inns, too, are taking, and how many fields and meadows! but as places of passage merely. You have an object, which is this: to get home, to do your duty to your family, friends, and fellow-countrymen, to attain inward freedom, serenity, happiness, contentment. Style takes your fancy, arguing takes your fancy, and you forget your home and want to make your abode with them and to stay with them, on the plea that they are taking. Who denies that they are taking? but as places of passage, as inns. And when I say this, you suppose me to be attacking the care for style, the care for argument. I am not; I attack the resting in them, the not looking to the end which is beyond them.'

Now, when we come across a poet like Théophile Gautier, we have a poet who has taken up his abode at an inn, and never got farther. There may be inducements to this or that one of us, at this or that moment, to find delight in him, to cleave to him; but after all, we do not change the truth about him, – we only stay ourselves in his inn along with him. And when we come across a poet like Wordsworth, who sings:

> Of truth, of grandeur, beauty, love and hope,
> And melancholy fear subdued by faith,
> Of blessed consolations in distress,
> Of moral strength and intellectual power,
> Of joy in widest commonalty spread –

then we have a poet intent on 'the best and master thing', and who prosecutes his journey home. We say, for brevity's sake that he deals with *life*, because he deals with that in which life really consists. This is what Voltaire means to praise in the

English poets, – this dealing with what is really life. But always it is the mark of the greatest poets that they deal with it; and to say that the English poets are remarkable for dealing with it, is only another way of saying what is true, that in poetry the English genius has especially shown its power.

Wordsworth deals with it, and his greatness lies in his dealing with it so powerfully. I have named a number of celebrated poets above all of whom he, in my opinion, deserves to be placed. He is to be placed above poets like Voltaire, Dryden, Pope, Lessing, Schiller, because these famous personages with a thousand gifts and merits, never, or scarcely ever, attain the distinctive accent and utterance of the high and genuine poets:

Quique pii vates et Phoebo digna-locuti.

at all. Burns, Keats, Heine, not to speak of others in our list, have this accent; – who can doubt it? And at the same time they have treasures of humour, felicity, passion, for which in Wordsworth we shall look in vain. Where, then, is Wordsworth's superiority? It is here; he deals with more of *life* than they do; he deals with *life*, as a whole, more powerfully.

No Wordsworthian will doubt this. Nay the fervent Wordsworthian will add, as Mr Leslie Stephen does, that Wordsworth's poetry is precious because his philosophy is sound; that his 'ethical system is as distinctive and capable of exposition as Bishop Butler's, that his poetry is informed by ideas which fall spontaneously into a scientific system of thought'. But we must be on our guard against the Wordsworthians, if we want to secure for Wordsworth his due rank as a poet. The Wordsworthians are apt to praise him for the wrong things, and to lay far too much stress upon what they call his philosophy. His poetry is the reality, his philosophy – so far, at least, as it may put on the form and habit of 'a scientific system of thought', and the more that it puts them on, – is the illusion. Perhaps we shall one day learn to make this proposition general, and to say: Poetry is the reality, philosophy, the illusion. But in Wordsworth's case at any rate, we cannot do him justice until we dismiss his formal philosophy.

The Excursion abounds with philosophy, and therefore *The Excursion* is to the Wordsworthian what it can never be to the disinterested lover of poetry, – a satisfactory work. 'Duty exists,' says Wordsworth, in *The Excursion;* and then he proceeds thus:

> ... Immutably survive,
> For our support, the measures and the forms,
> Which an abstract intelligence supplies,
> Whose kingdom is, where time and space are not.

And the Wordsworthian is delighted, and thinks here is a sweet union of philosophy and poetry. But the disinterested lover of poetry will feel that the lines carry us really not a step farther than the proposition which they would interpret; that they are a tissue of elevated but abstract verbiage, alien to the very nature of poetry.

Or let us come direct to the centre of Wordsworth's philosophy, as 'an ethical system, as distinctive and capable of systematical exposition as Bishop Butler's':

> ... One adequate support
> For the calamities of mortal life
> Exists, one only, – an assured belief
> That the procession of our fate, howe'er
> Sad or disturbed, is ordered by a Being
> Of infinite benevolence and power;
> Whose everlasting purposes embrace
> All accidents, converting them to good.

That is doctrine such as we hear in church too, religious and philosophic doctrine; and the attached Wordsworthian loves passages of such doctrine, and brings them forward in proof of his poet's excellence. But however true the doctrine may be, it has, as here presented, none of the characters of *poetic* truth, the kind of truth which we require from a poet, and in which Wordsworth is really strong.

Even the 'intimations' of the famous Ode, those corner-stones of the supposed philosophic system of Wordsworth – the idea of the high instincts and affections coming out in childhood, testifying of a divine home recently left, and fading away as our life proceeds, – this idea, of undeniable beauty as a play of fancy, has itself not the character of poetic truth of the best kind; it has no real solidity. The instinct of delight in Nature and her beauty had no doubt extraordinary strength in Wordsworth himself as a child. But to say that universally this instinct is mighty in childhood, and tends to die away afterwards, is to say what is extremely doubtful. In many people, perhaps with the majority of educated persons, the love of nature is nearly imperceptible at ten years old, but strong and operative at thirty. In general we may say of these high instincts of early childhood, the base of the alleged systematic philosophy of Wordsworth, what Thucydides says of the early achievements of the Greek race: 'It is impossible to speak with certainty of what is so remote; but from all that we can really investigate I should say that they were no very great things.'

Finally, the 'scientific system of thought' in Wordsworth gives us at last such poetry as this, which the devout Wordsworthian accepts:

> O for the coming of that glorious time
> When, prizing knowledge as her noblest wealth
> And best protection, this Imperial Realm,
> While she exacts allegiance, shall admit
> An obligation, on her part, to *teach*
> Them who are born to serve her and obey;
> Binding herself by statute to secure,
> For all the children whom her soil maintains,
> The rudiments of letters, and inform
> The mind with moral and religious truth.

Wordsworth calls Voltaire dull, and surely the production of these un-Voltairian lines must have been imposed on him as a judgment! One can hear them being quoted at a Social Science Congress; one can call up the whole scene. A great room in one of our dismal provincial towns; dusty air and jaded afternoon daylight; benches full of men with bald heads and women in spectacles; an orator lifting up his face from a manuscript written within and without to declaim these lines of Wordsworth; and in the soul of any poor child of nature who may have wandered in thither, an unutterable sense of lamentation, and mourning, and woe!

'But turn we,' as Wordsworth says, 'from these bold, bad

men', the haunters of Social Science Congresses. And let us be on our guard, too, against the exhibitors and extollers of a 'scientific system of thought' in Wordsworth's poetry. The poetry will never be seen aright while they thus exhibit it. The cause of its greatness is simple, and may be told quite simply. Wordsworth's poetry is great because of the extraordinary power with which Wordsworth feels the joy offered to us in nature, the joy offered to us in the simple primary affections and duties; and because of the extraordinary power with which, in case after case, he shows us this joy, and renders it so as to make us share it.

The source of joy from which he thus draws is the truest and most unfailing source of joy accessible to man. It is also accessible universally. Wordsworth brings us word, therefore, according to his own strong and characteristic line, he brings us word

Of joy in widest commonalty spread,

Here is an immense advantage for a poet. Wordsworth tells of what all seek, and tells of it at its truest and best source, and yet a source where all may go and draw for it.

Nevertheless, we are not to suppose that everything is precious which Wordsworth, standing even at this perennial and beautiful source, may give us. Wordsworthians are apt to talk as if it must be, they will speak with the same reverence of *The Sailor's Mother*, for example, as of *Lucy Gray*. They do their master harm by such lack of discrimination. *Lucy Gray* is a beautiful success; *The Sailor's Mother* is a failure. To give aright what he wishes to give, to interpret and render success-fully, is not always within Wordsworth's own command. It is within no poet's command; here is part of the Muse, the inspiration, the God, the 'not ourselves'. In Wordsworth's case, the accident, for so it may almost be called, of inspiration, is of peculiar importance. No poet, perhaps, is so evidently filled with a new and sacred energy when the inspiration is upon him; no poet, when it fails him is so left 'weak as is a breaking wave'. I remember hearing him say that Goethe's poetry was not inevitable enough. The remark is striking and true; no line in Goethe, as Goethe said himself, but its maker knew well how it came there. Wordsworth is right, Goethe's poetry is not inevitable; not inevitable enough. But Wordsworth's poetry, when he is at his best, is inevitable, as inevitable as Nature herself. It might seem that Nature not only gave him the matter for his poem, but wrote his poem for him. He has no style. He was too conversant with Milton not to catch at times his master's manner, and he has fine Miltonic lines; but he has no assured poetic style of his own, like Milton. When he seeks to have a style he falls into ponderosity and pomposity. In *The Excursion* we have his style, as an artistic product of his own creation; and although Jeffrey completely failed to recognise Wordsworth's real greatness, he was yet not wrong in saying of *The Excursion*, as a work of poetic style: 'This will never do'. And yet magical as is that power, which Wordsworth has not, of assured and possessed poetic style, he has something which is an equivalent for it.

Every one who has any sense for these things feels the subtle turn, the heightening, which is given to a poet's verse by his genius for style. We can feel it in the

> After life's fitful fever, he sleeps well –

of Shakespeare; in the

> ...though fall'n on evil days,
> On evil days though fall'n, and evil tongues –

of Milton. It is the incomparable charm of Milton's power of poetic style which gives such worth to *Paradise Regained*, and makes a great poem of a work in which Milton's imagination does not soar high. Wordsworth has in constant possession, and at command, no style of this kind; but he had too poetic a nature, and had read the great poets too well, not to catch, as I have already remarked, something of it occasionally. We find it not only in his Miltonic lines; we find it in such a phrase as this, where the manner is his own, not Milton's:

> ...the fierce confederate storm
> Of sorrow barricadoed evermore
> Within the walls of cities;

although even here, perhaps, the power of style which is un-
deniable, is more properly that of eloquent prose than the subtle
heightening and change wrought by genuine poetic style. It is
style, again, and the elevation given by style, which chiefly
makes the effectiveness of *Laodameia*. Still the right sort of
verse to choose from Wordsworth, if we are to seize his true
and most characteristic form of expression, is a line like this
from *Michael*:

And never lifted up a single stone

There is nothing subtle in it, no heightening, no study of poetic
style, strictly so called, at all; yet it is expression of the highest
and most truly expressive kind. Wordsworth owed much to
Burns, and a style of perfect plainness, relying for effect solely
on the weight and force of that which with entire fidelity it
utters, Burns could show him.

> The poor inhabitant below
> Was quick to learn and wise to know,
> And keenly felt the friendly glow
> And softer flame;
> But thoughtless follies laid him low
> And stain'd his name.

Every one will be conscious of a likeness here to Wordsworth;
and if Wordsworth did great things with this nobly plain
manner, we must remember, what indeed he himself would
always have been forward to acknowledge, that Burns used it
before him.

Still Wordsworth's use of it has something unique and
unmatchable. Nature herself seems, I say, to take the pen out of
his hand, and to write for him with her own bare, sheer, pene-
trating power. This arises from two causes; from the profound
sincereness with which Wordsworth feels his subject, and also
from the profoundly sincere and natural character of his subject
itself. He can and will treat such a subject with nothing but the
most plain, first-hand, almost austere naturalness. His expres-
sion may often be called bald, as, for instance, in the poem of
Resolution and Independence; but is bald as the bare mountain tops
are bald, with a baldness which is full of grandeur.

Whenever we meet with the successful balance, in Words-
worth, of profound truth of subject with profound truth of
execution, he is unique. His best poems are those which most
perfectly exhibit this balance. I have a warm admiration for
Laodameia and for the great Ode; but if I am to tell the very
truth, I find *Laodameia* not wholly free from something artificial,
and the great Ode not wholly free from something declamatory.
If I had to pick out poems of a kind most perfectly to show
Wordsworth's unique power, I should rather choose poems
such as *Michael, The Fountain, The Highland Reaper*. And poems
with the peculiar and unique beauty which distinguishes these,
Wordsworth produced in considerable number; besides very
many other poems of which the worth, although not so rare as
the worth of these, is still exceedingly high.

On the whole, then, as I said at the beginning, not only is
Wordsworth eminent by reason of the goodness of his best
work, but he is eminent also by reason of the great body of good
work which he has left to us. With the ancients I will not com-
pare him. In many respects the ancients are far above us, and
yet there is something that we demand which they can never
give. Leaving the ancients, let us come to the poets and poetry
of Christendom. Dante, Shakespeare, Molière, Milton, Goethe,
are altogether larger and more splendid luminaries in the
poetical heaven than Wordsworth. But I know not where else,
among the moderns, we are to find his superiors.

To disengage the poems which show his power, and to
present them to the English-speaking public and to the world,
is the object of this volume. I by no means say that it contains
all which in Wordsworth's poems is interesting. Except in the
case of *Margaret*, a story composed separately from the rest of
The Excursion, and which belongs to a different part of England,
I have not ventured on detaching portions of poems, or on
giving any piece otherwise than as Wordsworth himself gave
it. But under the conditions imposed by this reserve, the volume
contains, I think, everything, or nearly everything, which may
best serve him with the majority of lovers of poetry, nothing
which may disserve him.

I have spoken lightly of Wordsworthians; and if we are to
get Wordsworth recognised by the public and by the world,

we must recommend him not in the spirit of a clique, but in the spirit of disinterested lovers of poetry. But I am a Wordsworthian myself. I can read with pleasure and edification *Peter Bell*, and the whole series of *Ecclesiastical Sonnets*, and the address to Mr Wilkinson's spade, and even the *Thanksgiving Ode*, – everything of Wordsworth, I think, except *Vaudracour and Julia*. It is not for nothing that one has been brought up in the veneration of a man so truly worthy of homage; that one has seen him and heard him, lived in his neighbourhood, and been familiar with his country. No Wordsworthian has a tenderer affection for this pure and sage master than I, or is less really offended by his defects. But Wordsworth is something more than the pure and sage master of a small band of devoted followers, and we ought not to rest satisfied until he is seen to be what he is. He is one of the very chief glories of English Poetry; and by nothing is England so glorious as by her poetry. Let us lay aside every weight which hinders our getting him recognised as this, and let our one study be to bring to pass, as widely as possible and as truly as possible, his own word concerning his poems: 'They will co-operate with the benign tendencies in human nature and society, and will, in their degree, be efficacious in making men wiser, better, and happier.'

[Essays in Criticism]

SWINBURNE

IT DOES not seem to me that the highest distinctive qualities of
Wordsworth's genius are to be found in what is usually con-
sidered his most characteristic work. In homely accuracy and
simplicity he is equalled by Cowper and distanced by Burns: for
the great Scotchman is not more certainly his superior in
humour, animation, and variety than in vivid veracity of accurate
and sympathetic representation. Few poets were ever less realis-
tic than Milton: few at least ever depended less on accuracy of
transcription from the simple truth and modesty of nature for
the accomplishment of their highest and most abiding aims: and
yet the place of Wordsworth, whose own professed aim was to
study and to reproduce in the effects of his verse the effects of
nature in their most actual simplicity, is rather with Milton or
with Pindar than with Cowper or with Burns. He wants indeed
the constancy of impulse, the certitude of achievement, the
steadfastness of inspiration, by which Pindar and Milton are
exalted and sustained through the whole course of their spiritual
flight from summit to summit of majestic imagination and moral
ardour; their sovereign sway and masterdom lay hardly within
reach of his less imperial spirit; the ethics of Wordsworth are
scarcely so solid and profound as theirs, so deeply based on
righteousness and reality, on principles of truth and manhood
invariable and independent of custom or theology, of tradition
and of time. But is there anything in modern poetry so Pindaric
– in other words, is there anything at once so exalted and so
composed, so ardent and serene, so full of steadfast light and the
flameless fire of imaginative thought, as the hymn which assigns
to the guardianship of duty or everlasting law the fragrance of
the flowers on earth and the splendour of the stars in heaven?
Here at least his conception of duty, of righteousness, and of
truth is one with the ideal of Aeschylus, of Alighieri and of
Hugo: no less positive and pure, no more conventional or acci-
dental than is theirs. And in a lesser lyric than this we find the same
spontaneous and sublime perfection of inspired workmanship.

[113]

None but a poet of the first order could have written the eight lines in which the unforeseeing security of a charmed and confident happiness is opposed to the desolate certitude of unforeseen bereavement by a single touch of contrast, a single note of comparison, as profound in its simplicity as the deepest wellspring of human emotion or remembrance itself. No elaboration of elegiac lament could possibly convey that sense of absolute and actual truth, of a sorrow set to music of its own making, – a sorrow hardly yet wakened out of wonder into sense of its own reality, – which is impressed at once for ever on the spirit of any reader, at any age, by those eight faultless and incomparable verses.

As the poet of high-minded loyalty to his native land, Wordsworth stands alone above all his compeers and successors: royalist and conservative as he appeared, he never really ceased, while his power of song was unimpaired, to be in the deepest and most literal sense a republican; a citizen to whom the commonweal – the 'common good of all', for which Shakespeare's ideal patriot shed Cæsar's blood less willingly than his own – was the one thing worthy of any man's and all men's entire devotion. The depth and intensity, the fixity and the fervour of his interest in personal suffering and individual emotion did but help to build up, to fortify and consolidate, this profound and lofty patriotism. But in what we may call his more private capacity as a poet the most especial and distinctive quality of his genius is rather its pathetic than its introspective, its tragic than its philosophic note. A poet of action he never claimed or wished to be: as a poet of introspection, of spiritual insight or ethical doctrine, he has been – if it may be said without irreverence – perhaps alike overrated by others and by himself: but as the poet of suffering, and of sympathy with suffering, his station is unequalled in its kind. Here, except when he is floated away on the unconfined and wide-weltering waters of his limitless blank verse, he scarcely ever seems to me – as even to Mr Arnold I find that he sometimes seems – to go wrong. Like those English settlers in Ireland who became *ipsis Hibernis Hiberniores*, I find myself on this point more Wordsworthian than the most eminent of contemporary Wordsworthians. He complains that his fellow disciples 'will speak with the same reverence of *The Sailor's Mother*, for example, as of *Lucy Gray*.

They do their master harm by such lack of discrimination. *Lucy Gray* is a beautiful success: *The Sailor's Mother* is a failure.' To me I must admit that it seems the finer success of the two: the deeper in its pathos, the more enduring in its effect, the happier if also the more venturous in its simplicity.

But on the other hand Mr Arnold places at the close of the narrative poems elected by him for especial honour, as a crowning example of Wordsworth's excellence in that line, the first book of *The Excursion*, detached from the others and presented under the title of *Margaret* as a separate and independent idyll, side by side with the faultless and ever memorable poem of *Michael*. It is through no pleasure in contradiction but with genuine reluctance to differ from the majority of Wordsworth's ablest and most sympathetic admirers, that I say what I have always thought, when I avow an opinion that as surely as *Michael* is a beautiful success *Margaret* is a failure. Its idyllic effect is not heightened but impaired by the semi-dramatic form of narrative – a form so generally alien to Wordsworth's genius that its adoption throughout so great a part of *The Excursion* would of itself suffice at once to establish and to explain the inferiority of that poem to *The Prelude*. But in this particular instance the narrative drags even more heavily than in the case which affords Mr Arnold a single exception to his practical rule of universal tolerance or enjoyment. He can read, he tells us, with pleasure and edification, everything of Wordsworth, except *Vaudracour and Julia*. Certainly that episode is a somewhat 'heavy-gaited' and torpid offspring of the poet's blameless Muse: but this is not the only occasion on which she seems to stand sorely in need of a shove from some critical Baxter of more potent and more dexterous hand than Jeffrey. Whatever of interest or pathos there may be in the Wanderer's record of Margaret's troubles is fairly swamped in a watery world of words as monotonous and colourless as drizzling mist. The story would be sad enough, if there were any story to tell: and Wordsworth, in his 'wiser mind', might have turned the subject to some elegiac account: but all the main effect – in spite of certain details and certain passages or phrases impossible to any but a master of pathetic emotion – is washed away by the drowsy and dreary overflow of verses without limit or landmark. The

truth is that Wordsworth, of all poets worthy to be named in
the same day with him, stood the most in need of artificial con-
finement and support to prevent his work from sprawling into
shapeless efflorescence and running to unprofitable seed; though,
if any one were to speak of his blank verse in a tone of sweeping
and intemperate irreverence, no doubt the great names of
Lorton Vale and Tintern Abbey would rise up before all our
memories to shame the speaker into silence; Milton alone could
surpass, perhaps Milton alone has equalled, the very finest work
of his great disciple in this majestic kind: the music of some few
almost incomparable passages seems to widen and deepen the
capacity of the sense for reception and enjoyment and under-
standing of the sublimest harmonies. And outside the range of
blank verse it is not of Milton only that the genius of Words-
worth at its highest should remind us; it is not with Milton's
only that this genius may profitably be compared. Wordsworth,
says Mr Arnold, is not of the same order with the great poets
who made such verse as he takes to represent at its best and
highest the special genius, the typical force, of Homer, of Dante,
or of Shakespeare. A poet of the same order with these, or with
such sovereign masters of lyric style as Pindar and Coleridge
and Shelley, he may not be – I should say myself that he most
unquestionably was not; but if we look to detached lines and
phrases, – a method greatly favoured and skillfully practised by
Mr Arnold, – there is no poet of any time or nation beside whom
Wordsworth need fear to stand. There is nothing of style, in
the highest sense, more Shakespearian in Shakespeare than such
a turn of expression as 'the engines of her pain, the tools that
shaped her sorrow'; there is nothing outside Aeschylus so
Aeschylean as the magnificent and daring accuracy of the single
epithet which brings before us a whole charge of storming
breakers as they crowd and crash upon each other. No type has
ever so well represented, none could possibly represent so well,
the furious confusion and the headlong pressure of their onset,
as that one word which makes us hear and see, across wind and
lightning, the very sound and likeness of the 'trampling waves'.
All that Wordsworth could do – and the author of *The Excursion*
could do much – to make us forget his genius is itself forgotten
when such a line, such a single phrase as this, revives in our

memory the vibration of its music, the illumination of its truth. Forty thousand Byrons could not, with all their quantity of fustian, make up the sum of poetic eloquence – an eloquence born of faithful and joyful insight, of fancy-fed but fervent loyalty to nature, and to the style whose art itself is nature – which is comprised in this one line of Wordsworth's. Nor need we look only to single lines or stanzas for proof of the poet's occasional or momentary equality with the greatest: the one little nameless poem to which I but now referred as incomparable has a lyric perfection and purity of ring not surpassed by any single note of Shelley's, with a depth and gravity of emotion suppressed in the very act of expression to which I can remember no parallel in the range of song. 'If I had,' as Mr Arnold puts it, 'to pick out poems of a kind most perfectly to show Wordsworth's unique power', I should choose this one of all his shorter lyrics as distinctly unequalled by any other of them for exaltation and condensation of strength: while among his longer poems I should find it 'hard – almost impossible' – to make so positive a choice. But assuredly I should place on the one hand the *Ode to Duty*, on the other hand the *Song at the Feast of Brougham Castle*, as instances of decisive and perfect success, high – upon the whole – above the *Ode on Intimations of Immortality*. That famous, ambitious, and occasionally magnificent poem – which by the way is no more an ode than it is an epic – reveals the partiality and inequality of Wordsworth's inspiration as unmistakably as its purity and its power. Five stanzas or sections – from the opening of the fifth to the close of the ninth – would be utterly above all praise, if the note they are pitched in were sustained throughout; but after its unspeakably beautiful opening the seventh stanza falls suddenly far down beneath the level of those five first lines, so superb in the majesty of their sweetness, the magnificence of their tenderness, that to have written but the two last of them would have added glory to any poet's crown of fame. The details which follow on the close of this opening cadence do but impair its charm with a sense of incongruous realism and triviality, to which the suddenly halting and disjointed metre bears only too direct and significant a correspondence. No poet, surely, ever 'changed his hand' with such inharmonious awkwardness, or 'checked his pride' with such unseasonable humility, as Wordsworth. He of all others should have been careful to eschew the lawless discord of Cowley's 'immetrical' irregularity; for to say the least, he had not enough of 'music in himself' to supply in any measure or degree whatever the lack of ordered rhythm and lyric-law. Coleridge alone of all our poets ever wrote a single poem of any length which was also a poem of even and harmonious excellence in that illegitimate and anarchic fashion – for method it is none; Dryden and Wordsworth alike, and Keats no less than Shelley, fell short of this unique and unqualified success; and even so great a poem as *Dejection* is certainly less great by far than the same poet's ode on France. But if any proof were needed by any human intelligence or any human ear of the necessity for a law of harmony, the advantage of a method and a principle in even the most 'unpremeditated art,' no better proof could be required than a comparison of the poem last named with the sister ode 'on the departing year,' or of the regular with the irregular lyrics in *Hellas* or *Prometheus Unbound*. And if even Shelley, and if even Coleridge himself, all but omnipotent gods of song and utterly unapproachable in masterdom of music as they were, could not do their very best when working without a limit and singing without a law, how much less could any such miracle be expected from the far less infallible voice, the far less wonder-working hand of Wordsworth?

In so short a poem as the address *To Hartley Coleridge, six years old*, irregularity has a charm of its own; but that incomparable little masterpiece makes no pretension to the structure of a regular ode; and in any case it could be no more than an exception which would prove the rule.

That unique power of which Mr Arnold speaks so happily and so truly is nowhere displayed in more absolute purity of perfection than in those divine and enchanting verses. The peculiar note of Wordsworth's genius at its very highest is that of sublimity in tenderness. On this point again we must look only to the very highest poets of all for a parallel to this great, though most unequal and uncertain, most lawless and irregular poet. The pathos of Homer and Aeschylus, of Shakespeare and Hugo, is not merely allied or associated with sublimity, it is itself sublime. Coleridge, a name second to none of all time for splendour and sweetness of inspiration, is tender and sublime alternately; Wordsworth at his best is sublime by the very force of his tenderness. And sometimes, even when no such profound note of emotion is touched as to evoke this peculiar sense of power, the utter sincerity and perfect singleness of heart and spirit by which that highest effect is elsewhere produced may be no less distinctly and no less delightedly recognised. This quality of itself is no doubt insufficient to produce any such effect; and Wordsworth, it may be confessed, was liable to failure as complete as might have been expected, when, having no other merit of subject or of treatment to rely on, he was content to rely on his sincerity and simplicity alone; with a result sometimes merely trivial and unmeritable, sometimes actually repulsive or oppressive. At other times again the success of his method, or rather perhaps the felicity of his instinct was no less absolute and complete, even when the homeliness or humility of the subject chosen would have seemed incompatible with loftiness of feeling or grandeur of style. All readers who know good work when they see it must appreciate the beauty of his *Tribute to the Memory of a Dog;* all must feel the truth and the sweetness of its simplicity; but hardly any, I should suppose, have perceived on a first reading how grand it is – how noble, how lofty, how exalted, is the tone of its emotion. Here is that very sublimity of tenderness which I have ventured to indicate as Wordsworth's distinctive and crowning quality: a quality with which no other poet could have imbued his verse on such a subject and escaped all risk of apparent incongruity or insincerity. To praise a poem of this class on the score of dignity would seem to imply its deficiency in the proper and necessary qualities of simplicity and tenderness; yet here the loftier quality seems to grow as naturally as a flower out of the homelier and humbler element of feeling and expression. . . .

. . . . .

. . . But only for an instant can it ever be forgotten or can it ever seem doubtful that to Wordsworth above all other poets might have been addressed that superb apostrophe:

Tu donnes pour mesure, en tes ardentes luttes,
À la hauteur des bonds la profondeur des chutes.

Every such instance of his inability to realise his favourite ideal of realism throws into more vivid relief his imperial mastery of command in a far higher field of art than this. The very year which produced such doleful examples of eccentricity in dullness – relieved by hardly a touch here and there of attentive tenderness and truth – as *The Thorn* and *The Idiot Boy*, produced also the imperishable poem on Tintern Abbey; a poem which wants but the excision of one or two futile phrases, the reconstruction of two or three nerveless lines, to make perfect and unquestionable the justice of its claim to be ranked with the most triumphant successes of English poetry. Again, among the *Memorials of a Tour in Scotland*, 1803, we find side by side the astonishing admonition 'to the sons of Burns' – astonishing no less for its unutterable platitude of expression than for the taste which could dictate such a style of address on such an occasion – and the four glorious poems which give back with such serene perfection of stately ease and high simplicity the very spirit of the Highlands in their severe peace and bright austerity of summer. In the lines *To a Highland Girl*, in *Glen Almain*, *Stepping Westward*, and *The Solitary Reaper*, the purest note of Wordsworth's genius is discernible in such fullness and sweetness of fervent thought and majestic sympathy, that the neighbourhood of any verse less noble than this is yet more inexplicable than regrettable. Two of these, *Glen Almain* and the *Reaper*, are throughout as perfect examples of the author's metrical instinct as of his peculiar tone of meditation; a point of as much or as little importance to a poet's work as is the command of line and colour to a painter's.

> He sang of battles, and the breath
> Of stormy war, and violent death –

there is a simple sounding couplet, with no very definable quality of musical expression in its cadence; yet the reader who should fail to recognise in it the distinguishing note of Wordsworth's power would at once prove himself incompetent as a judge of poetic style. And in such lines – austere, august, but sweet beyond the most polished and perfumed verse of any more obviously elaborate melodist – all the best poems representative of Wordsworth are rich enough to satisfy any taste unspoilt by too much indulgence in metrical confectionary. Wordsworth was so great a master of the strict and regular octosyllabic measure, that at times its proverbially 'fatal facility' seems in his hands alone to have lost all danger; its fluency gains strength and weight, its ease assumes gravity and grandeur. It is just and fit, therefore, that the noblest tribute ever paid to his name should be couched in verses not only worthy of his own hand, but written in this very simple and very exacting metre; so easy to work in badly, and so hard to work in well, that perhaps one poet alone has learnt all the effect of its elegiac resources from this master of the difficult and simple secret. Whether we do or do not agree at all points with the pupil as critic or commentator, it is none the less undeniable that the perfect, the final, the supreme praise of Wordsworth will always be sought, always cherished, and always enjoyed in Mr Arnold's memorial verses on his death. Here if anywhere is the right chord struck, the just and exact meed of honour assigned to a poet whose work was for so long the object of blundering blame and no less blundering praise. 'Wordsworth's healing power', his gift of direct or indirect refreshment, the comfort and support of his perfect and pure sincerity in all his dealings with nature, can best be felt, can only perhaps be felt in full, when we consent to forget and succeed in forgetting his excursion or excursions into the preacher's province, a territory dense and dubious with didactic quags and theosophic briars. In his own far loftier land of natural contemplation, when least meditative with any pre-pense or prefixed purpose, he could do such work and give such gifts as no other poet has given or has done. It was not when engaged in backing the Wanderer's moral paces against those of the heavily handicapped Solitary, or in reinforcing the verbose reiterations of that inexhaustible itinerant with the yet more indefatigable infecundity poured forth upon 'the pensive Sceptic' by 'the philosophic Priest', that Wordsworth was either a prophet or a poet. He sees deepest when he flies highest: and this, if I mistake not, is never in *The Excursion*, seldom in *The Prelude*, often in his earlier sonnets, and oftenest perhaps of all in such poems as partake almost equally of the lyric and the elegiac tone. In such a poem, for example, as *Resolution and*

Independence, there is a breath of prouder music, a ring of keener sound, than we expect or admit in elegy; it has more in its highest notes of the quality proper to lyric style – when the lyrist is likewise a thinker; to the lyric style of Sophocles or Pindar. And only in such work as the highest and rarest even of theirs may anyone think to find the like of such a verse as this:

The sleepless soul that perished in its pride.

I will back that against any of Mr Arnold's three representative quotations from Homer, from Dante, and from Shakespeare. It is like nothing from any other hand! the unspeakable greatness of its quality is Wordsworth's alone; and I doubt if it would really be as rash as it might seem to maintain that there is not and will never be a greater verse in all the world of song.

[*Miscellanies*]

LOWELL

THE NORMAL condition of many poets would seem to approach that temperature to which Wordsworth's mind could be raised only by the white heat of profoundly inward passion. And in proportion to the intensity needful to make his nature thoroughly aglow is the very high quality of his best verses. They seem rather the productions of nature than of man, and have the lastingness of such, delighting our age with the same startle of newness and beauty that pleased our youth. Is it his thought? It has the shifting inward lustre of diamond. Is it his feeling? It is as delicate as the impressions of fossil ferns. He seems to have caught and fixed for ever in immutable grace the most evanescent and intangible of our intuitions, the very ripple-marks on the remotest shores of being. But this intensity of mood which insures high quality is by its very nature incapable of prolongation, and Wordsworth, in endeavouring it, falls more below himself, and is, more even than many poets his inferiors in imaginative quality, a poet of passages.

. . . . .

But when, as I have said, our impartiality has made all those qualifications and deductions against which even the greatest poet may not plead his privilege, what is left to Wordsworth is enough to justify his fame. Even where his genius is wrapped in clouds, the unconquerable lightning of imagination struggles through, flashing out unexpected vistas, and illuminating the humdrum pathway of our daily thought with a radiance of momentary consciousness that seems like a revelation. If it be the most delightful function of the poet to set our lives to music, yet perhaps he will be even more sure of our maturer gratitude if he do his part also as moralist and philosopher to purify and enlighten; if he define and encourage our vacillating perceptions of duty; if he piece together our fragmentary apprehensions of our own life and that larger life whose unconscious instruments we are, making of the jumbled bits of our dissected map of experience a coherent chart. In the great poets there is an exquisite sensibility both of soul and sense that sympathises like gossamer sea-moss with every movement of the element in which it floats, but which is rooted on the solid rock of our common sympathies. Wordsworth shows less of this finer feminine fibre of organisation than one or two of his contemporaries, notably than Coleridge or Shelley; but he was a masculine thinker, and in his more characteristic poems there is always a kernel of firm conclusion from far-reaching principles that stimulates thought and challenges meditation. Groping in the dark passages of life, we come upon some axiom of his, as it were a wall that gives us our bearings and enables us to find an outlet. Compared with Goethe we feel that he lacks that serene impartiality of mind which results from breadth of culture; nay, he seems narrow, insular, almost provincial. He reminds us of those saints of Dante who gather brightness by revolving on their own axis. But through this very limitation of range he gains perhaps in intensity and the impressiveness which results from eagerness of personal conviction. If we read Wordsworth through, as I have just done, we find ourselves changing our mind about him at every other page, so uneven is he. If we read our favourite poems or passages only, he will seem uniformly great. And even as regards *The Excursion* we should remember how few long poems will bear consecutive reading. For my part I know of but one, – the *Odyssey*.

. . . . . .

None of our great poets can be called popular in any exact sense of the word, for the highest poetry deals with thoughts and emotions which inhabit, like rarest sea-mosses, the doubtful limits of that shore between our abiding divine and our fluctuating human nature, rooted in the one, but living in the other, seldom laid bare, and otherwise visible only at exceptional moments of entire calm and clearness. Of no other poet except Shakespeare have so many phrases become household words as of Wordsworth. If Pope has made current more epigrams of worldly wisdom, to Wordsworth belongs the nobler praise of having defined for us, and given us for a daily possession, those faint and vague suggestions of other-worldliness of whose gentle ministry with our baser nature the hurry and bustle of life scarcely ever allowed us to be conscious. He has won for himself a secure immortality by a depth of intuition which makes only the best minds at their best hours worthy, or indeed capable, of his companionship, and by a homely sincerity of human sympathy which reaches the humblest heart. Our language owes him gratitude for the habitual purity and abstinence of his style, and we who speak it, for having emboldened us to take delight in simple things, and to trust ourselves to our own instincts. And he hath his reward. It needs not to bid:

> Renowned Chaucer lie a thought more nigh
> To rare Beaumont, and learned Beaumont lie
> A little nearer Spenser;

for there is no fear of crowding in that little society with whom he is now enrolled as fifth in the succession of the great English Poets.

[Wordsworth]

WORDSWORTH AND HIS
TWENTIETH CENTURY CRITICS

No room for mourning: he's gone out
Into the noisy glen, or stands between the stones
Of the gaunt ridge, or you'll hear his shout
Rolling among the screes, he being a boy again.
He'll never fail nor die
And if they laid his bones
In the wet vaults or iron sarcophagi
Of fame, he'd rise at the first summer rain
And stride across the hills to seek
His rest among the broken lands and clouds.
He was a stormy day, a granite peak
Spearing the sky; and look, about its base
Words flower like crocuses in the hanging woods,
Blank though the dalehead and the bony face.

SIDNEY KEYES
from *William Wordsworth*

MURIEL SPARK

Introduction

MORE than is the case with most poets, Wordsworth the man and the poet are interdependent, and Wordsworthian criticism during the twentieth century has been marked by a narrowing of the distinction between the functions of biographer and literary critic. The researches of Professors Legouis and Harper into Wordsworth's stay in France during 1791-92, and the publication of Professor de Selincourt's *variorum* edition of the *Prelude*, have provided the main sources of fresh information that illuminate both Wordsworth's life and his work, for students of this century.

Before these discoveries were made known, the main trend of criticism on Wordsworth derived from the later nineteenth century critics, Arnold and Pater, and in 1909, Arthur Symons' approach to Wordsworth followed largely their line of thought, that the clue to Wordsworth lies in his work and in the poet's own formulae rather than in the outside events of his life.

'Sincerity was at the root of all Wordsworth's merits and defects; it gave him his unapproachable fidelity to nature, and also his intolerable fidelity to his own whims,' Arthur Symons wrote, with more accuracy than he could have been aware of. For if we have come to learn that sincerity, either in Words-worth's life or in his work, was not the prevailing factor, we know too, that it was sincerity to his own image in the eyes of man, that was at the root 'of all Wordsworth's merits and defects'.

It was not until 1922 that Professor Legouis was able to produce his *William Wordsworth and Annette Vallon* which, although not itself a critical work, proved a turning point in Wordsworthian criticism. The events outlined here are, briefly, that during Wordsworth's visit to France he had a love affair with a Frenchwoman, Annette Vallon, by whom he had a daughter; that he left France after the child was born having promised to return and marry Annette; that Annette Vallon came from a family whose sympathies were Royalist; and that later she herself became actively engaged in Royalist activities. Professor Legouis further showed that Wordsworth's poem, *Vaudracour and Julia*, contains much than can be related to the poet's association with Annette.

The publication, in 1916, of Professor de Selincourt's edition of the *Prelude*, gave rise to increased speculation on Wordsworth in the light of the Vallon episode, for here could be compared the variations of this poem, which, over a period of some thirty-five years, Wordsworth revised and redrafted. It is on the significance of Wordsworth's amendments, running parallel with the course of his life, that many modern critics have based their view of Wordsworth.

Now, Mr Eliot has said, very reasonably, '. . . the study of psychology has impelled men . . . to investigate the mind of the poet with a confident ease which has led to some fantastic excesses and aberrant criticism'. Aware of this danger, a number of contemporary critics have yet seen in Wordsworth a poet to whom the application of psychological treatment is supremely justified. For the first time in literature, this poet consciously wrote an account of his own life as a study of 'The Growth of a Poet's Mind', reciting, as it were, his own case history with about as much frankness and as much evasion as any psychologist will expect from the subject of his analysis. If ever a poet's work invited a psychological analysis, it is felt, that poet was Wordsworth; and his *Prelude* being, as Professor de Selincourt wrote, 'an essential living document for the interpretation of Wordsworth's life and poetry', it is natural that this poem, and Wordsworth's revision again and again, of it, should form a basis for research into its author's genius. Whereas the subject of psycho-analysis will return to his first statements and withdraw or amend them until the source of his conflict is recognised in those very deviations, Wordsworth, it is shown by his revisions of the *Prelude*, moved into a more complicated state (conditioned, as Mr Read sees it, by remorse). In Wordsworth's reversion of the usual order of the analytical process, can be traced the course of his decline as a poet.

One of the first to incorporate the new material was Professor Harper, when he revised his life of Wordsworth, first published in 1916. This work remains today the most comprehensive on the subject, and is the prototype in the history of Wordsworthian opinion, of the literary critical-biography. If Professor Harper does not express any strong, provocative theories, and if he is not, on the other hand, deeply intuitive or original, his view is a balanced one that may be said to represent, in general terms, the variety of opinion on the subject that has been produced in the last twenty years.

In 1923, Professor H. W. Garrod followed this start in the literary biographical critical method, with a series of essays limited to an attentive examination of Wordsworth's work in the poet's supreme creative decade, between 1797 and 1807. Professor Garrod sets himself primarily to seek an explanation of Wordsworth's unevenness as a poet, to define the nature of his 'oasis of power and splendour amid endless tracts of middling performance'.

About the discovery of Wordsworth's relationship with Annette Vallon, Professor Garrod writes, 'Let us agree that this is startling, and that it compels us to look at Wordsworth in a new way. But it is not necessary that we should lose our heads.'

If Professor Garrod has kept his head entirely over the matter of Annette, it might seem that he has done so at the expense of sensibility to the nature of the poet. To believe that for 'Wordsworth, reviewing the history of his spiritual development [i.e., in *The Prelude*] the Annette episode did not present itself as a part of his life in which his passions and feelings had been seriously engaged', is to ignore the fact of Wordsworth's tampering and retampering with those portions of the *Prelude* which approximate to his experience with Annette. This is an isolated example of Professor Garrod's fairly consistent refusal to recognise the emotional forces in the poet's life, and their effect upon his poetry. To Professor Garrod, the intellectual stimuli of Wordsworth's early manhood are, however, of extreme significance, as when he tells us, 'Godwin's *Political Justice* was published in the same month [as Erasmus Darwin's *The Botanical Garden*]; and it was in this month also that war was declared between England and revolutionary France. These two events are of first-rate importance for Wordsworth's development, and their interconnexion requires explanation and emphasis.'

[131]

It seems to be a question here of whether the emotion pro-
duced in Wordsworth by his experience with Annette and the
birth of his daughter was of negligible importance, and that
produced by a new-found political faith, and its seeming betrayal
by England, was to Wordsworth of 'first-rate' importance.
Professor Garrod is perhaps forgetting that Wordsworth was
firstly a poet and afterwards a scholar and politician; and this
somewhat frigid conception of a poet's mind has possibly led
him to take *The Prelude* at its face value; to say, in fact, 'I am
disposed to feel that, in it, Wordsworth has tried to put to us
those parts of his experience which he believed, in a deep sense,
to *matter*. And in general I am inclined to the belief that, not
only are poets commonly a more truthful race than other men,
but they frequently understand themselves better than other
people come to understand them.'

To explain in what way the Annette episode *mattered* to
Wordsworth and his work, and to show that Wordsworth
understood himself perhaps too well for his own peace of mind,
or for the continued health of his poetry, was the purpose of the
next critical biography of Wordsworth to appear, in 1930, by
Mr Herbert Read.

So far as his work on Wordsworth is concerned, Mr Read's
attitude must be taken as that suggested by his words, 'I feel
that as human beings we enter the world with definite potentiali-
ties; and though our course in life is determined by the obstacles
we meet, it is only deflected in certain limited lateral directions.'
It is an approach wide enough to admit scope to his subject in
'certain limited lateral directions', and with Wordsworth, this
is an essential consideration, since he, of all people, responded
to his surroundings, was influenced mainly by the personalities
of others, was deflected from his course for better or worse,
by the obstacles he met. Mr Read confirms this point of view
when he speaks of the influence on Wordsworth of his revolu-
tionary companion in France, Beaupuy: 'Wordsworth was con-
verted, and once again we may note that it was not an act of
reason, but of faith. It was the personal contact with this
glowing sincerity in a man whom he could but admire that
aroused Wordsworth's enthusiasm for the rights of humanity.'
This aspect of Wordsworth, Mr Read sees as leading to his

change of political faith. 'Within five years,' Mr Read tells us, 'he had rejected the intellect and all its works, and fallen back on his original faith in feeling and intuition and the all-sufficiency of a direct contact with Nature. Wordsworth's mind . . . rejected the didactic teachings of books; he was influenced during the course of his life entirely through the medium of personality.' This argument tends towards a conception of Wordsworth's revolutionary phase as one superimposed upon the innate mentality of the man, and his later renunciation of that phase, not as apostacy, but as a reversion to the instinctive ideology of the Cumberland peasantry – a community of a highly stabilised, independent and by no means revolutionary nature.

It may be thought, then, that Mr Read's further assumption that Wordsworth's change of political attitude is bound up with Annette – she representing an association, in Wordsworth's mind, with France, to the extent of becoming a symbol of *revolutionary* France – is both redundant and questionable. Especially is this so, since Annette's family had Royalist sympathies, and by the time of Wordsworth's final break with her, she was actively and dangerously engaged in Royalist intrigue. (Indeed, in the following pages George Woodcock suggests that, because of the Vallon family's political ideas, Wordsworth may well have concealed his new faith from Annette.) The question of how far the conception of Annette *as a Royalist* had penetrated Wordsworth's unconscious mind, must therefore be weighed against the probability that his image of Annette was connected with the France that was, to Wordsworth, a clear revolutionary symbol.

Mr Read's theory of Wordsworth's remorse (arising from his desertion of Annette and his child), by which the decline of Wordsworth's poetic powers is attributed to the corrosion of guilt in a mind where memory played no small part, would seem to offer an answer to the problem of his poetic atrophy, which has only evoked one other serious solution.

To the Radical Romantic critics of Wordsworth, the desiccation of the poet's imaginative faculty is referred to his change of political attitude. The defect in this argument, it might be felt, is that it considers Wordsworth the poet to have been

[133]

primarily motivated, not by emotional but by intellectual causes. It is true that certain of these critics consider the impact of the French Revolution on Wordsworth, to have been principally of an emotional nature; but here one must be careful to distinguish between the emotions generated by ideas and principles, and those arising, in the more natural course of things, from human and personal relationships. From the evidence of experimental psychology, it would appear more likely that Wordsworth, as belonging to the species of the artist, should react, on the whole, to emotional stimuli of a physical, erotic and subjective nature.

Mr Read's theory, which he fortifies with evidence from Wordsworth's life and work, as well as with psychological evidence from a professional quarter (in the 1948 edition of his *Wordsworth*), has met with some criticism, but has yet to be superseded by an equally convincing explanation of Wordsworth's decline.

In 1930, when Mr Read's book first appeared, Mr William Empson, in his volume *Seven Types of Ambiguity*, was making quite a different approach to the poet, by concentrating on the specific and literal content of Wordsworth's poetry. Mr Empson takes the poem *Tintern Abbey* as an example to illustrate the situation 'when two or more meanings of a statement do not agree among themselves, but combine to make clear a more complicated state of mind in the author'.

In Wordsworth's case, Mr Empson makes the claim, 'the degree of pantheism implied by some of [his] most famous passages depends very much on the taste of the reader, who can impose grammar without difficulty to uphold his own views', and points out that when the reader tries to extract a philosophical standpoint, he is impeded by points of grammar which Mr Empson proceeds to enumerate.

Now this attitude, whilst eminently a close and critical one, may seem to be remarkably isolated from other considerations, such as Wordsworth's tendency to subordinate the meaning of a passage to its context and his lack of scruple to insert a word as a makeweight for metre or rhyme, irrespective of its precision as to meaning. So that, when Wordsworth composed the passage which so worries Mr Empson:

> And I have felt
> A presence that disturbs me with the joy
> Of elevated thoughts; a sense sublime
> Of something far more deeply interfused,
> Whose dwelling is the light of setting suns,
> And the round ocean, and the living air,
> And the blue sky, and in the mind of man...

one feels that he obviously inserted the word 'in' before the phrase, 'the mind of man' simply for the sake of metre, and intending no distinction, as Mr Empson suspects there is, between 'the mind of man' and 'the light'. In fact, this sort of isolated, microscopic criticism can hardly be said to be salutary to a deeper appreciation of Wordsworth, for, as my colleague Derek Stanford has pointed out, everyone knew what this passage meant until Mr Empson drew attention to the grammar.

Mr Aldous Huxley's approach to Wordsworth, in his essay *Wordsworth in the Tropics*, is characteristically fresh. Wordsworth, he says, secure in his Windermere haunts, never truly apprehended the diabolical attributes of nature, nor its fundamental alieny from the human state. 'A few weeks in Malaya or Borneo,' Mr Huxley asserts, 'would have undeceived him. Wandering in the hothouse darkness of the jungle, he would not have felt so serenely certain of those "Presences of Nature", those "Souls of Lonely Places", which he was in the habit of worshipping on the shores of Windermere and Rydal. The sparse inhabitants of the equatorial forest are all believers in devils.'

Mr Huxley sees a limitation in the Wordsworthian attitude to nature, in that it is applicable only to a country where nature has been subjugated by man. It may seem, however, that Mr Huxley has overlooked that this 'limitation' is a fairly wide one, that would obtain in the consideration of most European poets and their conception of nature; after all, Wordsworth did not address his words to the natives of New Guinea, any more than did Milton, for example.

The second 'defect' which Mr Huxley points out in the Wordsworthian conception of nature, he describes as being 'only possible for those who are prepared to falsify their immediate intuitions of Nature. For Nature, even in the temperate zone, is always alien and inhuman, and occasionally diabolic'. In so far as Mr Huxley notes the peculiar situation whereby Wordsworth 'will not admit that a yellow primrose is simply a yellow primrose – beautiful, but essentially strange, having its own alien life apart' but 'wants it to possess some sort of soul, to exist humanly, not simply flowerily,' he is making an acceptable, though not entirely original, observation on Wordsworth's approach to nature; but when the critic defines this particular approach as a 'defect,' he would seem to be self-condemned, since in so saying he is not prepared to allow the 'otherness' of the poet. – It is precisely because Wordsworth endowed nature with moral properties, that we appreciate this aspect of his poetry for (to use Mr Huxley's terminology) its Wordsworthness.

Mr Huxley makes an effective point in relating Wordsworth's apostasy to a change in his attitude towards Nature, when he tells us, 'He preferred, in the interests of a preconceived religious theory, to ignore the disquieting strangeness of things, to interpret the impersonal diversity of Nature in terms of a divine anglican unity.' But this is perhaps, to find in Wordsworth's later attitude to nature something rather different to the change that actually did take place. Wordsworth, even in his early days, was not remarkably aware of 'the disquieting *strangeness* of things'. Rather was the change in his outlook manifest in his different interpretations of the *unity of things;* for whereas in his first experience of nature, Wordsworth felt a pagan unity, his later attitude substituted an anglican conception of this unity.

Nor can we be entirely convinced when Mr Huxley suggests that 'a few months in the jungle would have cured him of his too easy and comfortable pantheism', and the present writer is obliged to John Heath-Stubbs for pointing out that Wordsworth, in his poem *Ruth*, anticipated such a criticism.

In 1932, Mr T. S. Eliot, in his volume *The Use of Poetry and the Use of Criticism*, published an essay on Wordsworth and Coleridge in which he reviewed the essential differences between the two poets whose names are inevitably linked, with especial reference to their work as critics. Here Mr Eliot shows that the differences reside in 'not only the men themselves, but the circumstances and motives of the composition of their principal critical statements', and that Wordsworth 'was of an opposite poetic type to Coleridge'.

But their difference extended further than that, Mr Eliot tells us, and here he makes a statement that has since proved somewhat disconcerting to many of his readers. Whereas Coleridge, he says, was a man who had come to acknowledge his wasted powers – a 'haunted man', Wordsworth, on the other hand, 'had no ghastly shadows at his back, no Eumenides to pursue him; or if he did, he gave no sign and took no notice'.

Now, up to this point in the criticism of this century, many had come to assume that Wordsworth, of all poets, was an exceptionally haunted man, pursued by Eumenides of a particularly avenging order. But Mr Eliot's qualifications might well be studied. If the Eumenides pursued Wordsworth, he asserts, 'he gave no sign and took no notice; and he went on droning the still sad music of infirmity to the verge of the grave'. It is indeed true that Wordsworth never faced his Eumenides in the way that Coleridge had done, and this fact brings us to the question of whether a man can be said to be haunted unless he is *conscious* of being haunted. One may incline to think not; and Wordsworth, as we know, took especial care that his conscious mind should not recognise the Eumenides.

We might be misguided, therefore, by looking upon Mr Eliot's statement as a direct antithesis to the prevalent view of Wordsworth which had been synthesised by Mr Read; and so far as the observation illustrates a fundamental difference between Wordsworth and Coleridge, it is an illuminating one.

Mr Eliot places especial stress on the difference between the two poets 'because their critical statements must be read together . . . Wordsworth wrote his *Preface* to defend his own manner of writing poetry, and Coleridge wrote the *Biographia* to defend Wordsworth's poetry; or in part he did'. There is a distinction here which deserves careful attention: the *Preface* was a defence of Wordsworth's *theory*; the *Biographia Literaria* contained a defence of Wordsworth's *poetry*. Coleridge, in fact, did not associate himself with the theories of Wordsworth, and actually made this clear – a fact which is difficult to reconcile with Mr Eliot's further statement that Coleridge and Wordsworth made 'common cause' of 'their new theory of poetic diction'; although it is possible that Mr Eliot interprets Coleridge's participation in the *Lyrical Ballads* as acquiescence to the doctrines expressed in its preface.

In his consideration of Wordsworth's theory, Mr Eliot reminds us that Wordsworth's innovations in poetic diction did not, in fact, originate with Wordsworth, who, 'when he said that his purpose was "to imitate, and as far as possible, to adopt, the very language of men", was only saying in other words what Dryden had said, and fighting the battle which Dryden had fought'.

'What, then,' asks Mr Eliot, 'was all the fuss about?'

'. . . it is Wordsworth's social interest,' he goes on to suggest, 'that inspires his own novelty of form in verse, and backs up his explicit remarks upon poetic diction; and it is really this social interest which (consciously or not) the fuss was all about.'

Whether or not one agrees that Dryden's object was one and the same with Wordsworth's, or that, had Dryden's social ethos been the same as Wordsworth's, Dryden's object would have produced a like effect, Mr Eliot's general theory must be considered a valuable contribution to Wordsworthian opinion when he draws attention to the relationship between the poet's social attitude and his trend of thought in formulating his theory. 'You cannot say,' Mr Eliot writes, 'that [Wordsworth's revolutionary faith] inspired his revolution in poetry, but it cannot be disentangled from the motives of his poetry. Any radical change in poetic form is likely to be the symptom of some very much deeper change in society and in the individual.' Thus, neither Dryden nor his contemporaries, however potent, could have been the vehicle for those symptoms which Wordsworth conveyed. One is led to suspect, however, that Mr Eliot's choice of parallel is not entirely unconditioned by his preference for non-romantic poetics.

In a separate essay (*Shelley and Keats*) Mr Eliot summarises his view that 'Wordsworth is really the first, in the unsettled state of affairs in his time, to annex new authority for the poet, to meddle with social affairs, and to offer a new kind of religious sentiment which it seemed the peculiar prerogative of the poet to interpret.'

Mr Hugh l'Anson Fausset's volume, *The Lost Leader*, which

was published in 1933, begins with a preface whose aims promise a stimulating study of Wordsworth. Here, we are told, Wordsworth is to be seen as 'the spiritual man striving and ultimately failing to be born out of the natural man'. All other critics, Mr Fausset feels, 'are partial or fail to go deep enough, because the critics have studied Wordsworth's life rather as an intellectual or psychological problem than as a spiritual event'. Mr Fausset does not, however, proceed to define his conception of the now ambiguous term 'spiritual', nor to distinguish between his conception of what is meant by 'spiritual', 'intellectual' and 'psychological'. But he goes on to explain, 'It was left to Blake, who never professed to be a critic, to make the simple and profound comment: "I see in Wordsworth," he said, "the natural man rising up against the spiritual man continually, and then he is no poet, but a heathen philosopher, at enmity with all true poetry and inspiration" . . . this book,' Mr Fausset continues, 'is nothing more nor less than an attempt to reveal in detail its truth.'

It might seem to some of Mr Fausset's readers that his choice of Blake as a motto-bearer, is inauspicious, since Blake, had the criteria for his judgment on Wordsworth been applied to his own poetry, would have come out about as favourably as has Mr Fausset from an application of his preface to his book.

Mr Fausset is of that school of critical biographers who like to intersperse their observations with such 'popular touches' as occur, for example, when we are told that Wordsworth 'lay in bed in a high room near the roof of his hotel, reading by candle-light', and one is moved to think that this sort of extraneous guess-work, whilst possibly encouraging the reader who knows nothing of Wordsworth, to learn something of the poet, cannot but impede the fulfilment of the author's expressed aims. Mr Fausset's conclusions, drawn from an attentive study of the *Prelude*, do not seem to vary, except in terminology, from those of Mr Read.

Mr F. R. Leavis's approach to Wordsworth is one of that category in which Mr Empson can be placed; it is a category distinguished from that of, for example, Mr Read, by its close attention to textual detail rather than to the circumstances surrounding a poet's work.

In his essay on Wordsworth, Mr Leavis observes that the poet had, 'if not a philosophy, a wisdom to communicate', his opinion being that Wordsworth's poetry invites attention to some philosophical content, but that 'when one does pay the necessary attention one always finds the kind of thing illustrated in Mr Empson's analysis', that is to say, contextual inconsistencies. Inconsistent, too, Mr Leavis asserts, is the admitted debt of Wordsworth's poetry to the philosophy of Hartley, although the technical phraseology of some passages suggest a debt to Hartley's associationism.

'Yet the burden of *The Prelude*,' Mr Leavis argues, 'is nevertheless, not essentially ambiguous, and Wordsworth's didactic offer was not merely empty self-delusion.' What he had to offer, Mr Leavis continues, was a way of life, 'his pre-occupation with sanity and spontaneity working at a level and in a spirit that it seems appropriate to call religious'. The critic carefully defines his use of the term 'religious' by drawing an unusual comparison: Wordsworth's preoccupation with 'a distinctively human naturalness, with sanity and spiritual health ... that of a mind intent always upon ultimate sanctions, and upon the living connexions between man and the extra-human universe', is, according to Mr Leavis, akin to Lawrence's pre-occupation with 'the deep levels, the springs, of life, the illimitable mystery that wells up into consciousness'.

The introduction of Lawrence into the argument is by no means an innocent one, for in doing so, Mr Leavis leads up to one of the most apparent differences between Wordsworth and Lawrence. Sex, says Mr Leavis, is an essential characteristic of the latter, whereas Wordsworth's poetry 'is remarkable for exhibiting the very opposite of such preoccupation'.

Now in pointing to this fact about Wordsworth's poetry, Mr Leavis indicates what some may regard as an abnormality in the poet's work. The examination, by other critics, of Wordsworth's life and mind, as well as of the passages in his poetry from which Wordsworth during his lifetime deliberately purged the erotic image, seems to suggest an abnormal repression of the erotic in his poetry. So that one may question Mr Leavis's reasoning when he writes, 'The pathological efficacy that Mr Read ascribed to the episode of Annette Vallon is discredited by the peculiarity just noted: such an absence of the erotic element hardly suggests repression.' Indeed, unless Mr Leavis is prepared to admit that an absence of the erotic element is normal; or alternatively that Wordsworth was a man of innate, and not superimposed, frigidity, it is difficult to see how the absence of eroticism in his verse can suggest anything but repression. In the former case, Mr Leavis is, of course, entitled to his opinion, although it is hardly to be supposed he holds it. If, on the other hand, his view is that Wordsworth was not naturally interested in sex, then Wordsworth's early life, and parts of the Prelude, tend to disprove it. It seems that the latter opinion is, in fact, Mr Leavis's, when he tells us that Wordsworth's 'various prose remarks about love plainly come from a mind that is completely free from timidity or uneasiness'. Wordsworth, of course, committed his erotic experiences, of which he came to feel somewhat ashamed, as little as possible to prose or poetry; but his *obiter dicta* as recorded by Carlyle and de Quincey, show clearly an attitude of disapproval towards manifestations of the erotic – an attitude that is commonly considered the outcome of repressed sexual instincts.

Since most critics would agree that there is a notable absence of sexual implications in Wordsworth's work, it may seem unnecessary to probe into the cause. But attached to the cause of this absence, is the question of whether it arises from repressed emotions, in which case the limitations of the poetry are likely to be greater than if it emanates from an uninhibited mind. In Mr Leavis's opinion, 'The absence no doubt constitutes a limitation, a restriction of interest; but it constitutes at the same time an aspect of Wordsworth's importance.' This aspect, Mr Leavis ingeniously shows, is revealed in Wordsworth's own *Preface*, where the poet's words imply 'spontaneity' which 'involves no cult of the instinctive and primitive at the expense of the rationalised and civilised'; the erotic, therefore, Mr Leavis associates with 'the instinctive and primitive' and not with the 'rationalised and civilised'. It is upon this equation that he takes his stand; and if we accept this principle, we shall be in a position to apprehend the critic's assertion, in spite of all he has said previously, that Wordsworth 'stands for a distinctly human naturalness'.

One of the most recent essays in Wordsworthian criticism by an eminent twentieth century critic, comes from Mr Middleton Murry in his *Coleridge and Wordsworth*. Mr Murry examines the relationship between the two poets, beyond the part played in it by Dorothy Wordsworth – whom Mr Eliot has designated the most important link between the two poets – and makes the point that, whilst it is not to be supposed that Wordsworth's and Coleridge's very different types of poetry emerged from their mutual relationship, 'it was Coleridge's response to [Wordsworth's] actual achievement which had brought them together. It was not until Coleridge attempted to put into practice the idea originating in the scheme of the *Lyrical Ballads*,' Mr Murry tells us, 'that the difference between Coleridge and Wordsworth became apparent.'

Wordsworth, Mr Murry sees as a man conditioned by a childhood 'both natural and ideal'; and Wordsworth saw in Coleridge 'a man who had been nurtured as a man should not be: a natural thing cruelly cut off from the sustenance of Nature, and withered'. Coleridge recognised this fact, and its implications – a difference in the approach of the two poets to everything including their work, this fundamental difference appearing 'in the very texture of the poetry of the two men'. According to Mr Murry, Wordsworth provided Coleridge with the material whereby he constructed his whole theory of Imagination; Wordsworth was the test for Coleridge's thought. Wordsworth's debt to Coleridge, on the other hand, was that 'Coleridge helped to make Wordsworth intellectually conscious of his own nature and his own achievement; and very probably he provided Wordsworth with a terminology'. In a later essay, however, Mr Murry suggests that Wordsworth's poetry suffered from his putting Coleridge's theory into practice, and that 'Coleridge should bear the chief responsibility for this contamination'.

The strength of Mr Murry's criticism is that he combines a close analysis of text with a wide view of all the circumstances surrounding it, in terms of its relation to the poet and to its situation in literature. If his latest work on Wordsworth – contained in his book *The Mystery of Keats* – is any criterion, this attitude might well influence a possible synthesis of two opposing schools of thought on Wordsworth.

As Wordsworthian opinion stands today, amongst the two main opposing groups of younger critics, namely those commonly known as neo-romantic and neo-classical, there would seem to be general agreement concerning the merits and defects of Wordsworth's verse throughout all stages of his career. But whereas the former have an answer to offer as to the reason for his poetic decline (that is, the repercussions of private remorse or of political apostasy), the latter appear to be lacking a solution.

JOHN HEATH-STUBBS

Wordsworth and Tradition

WE SPEAK of Wordsworth, and rightly, as the greatest of the English Romantic poets. But the term 'Romantic', as applied to a group or school of writers of the early nineteenth century, belongs, not to Wordsworth's own vocabulary, but to that of later critics and historians of literature. It is a useful label; but had Wordsworth known of it, and foreseen our use of it, I doubt if he would have been altogether happy in accepting our application of it to himself. The *Lyrical Ballads*, with the Preface to the Second Edition of 1800, were a manifesto, and we may regard them as having revolutionised the current conception of poetry. But neither Wordsworth nor Coleridge saw themselves as innovators, or as making a break with past traditions of poetry. Their appeal, rather, was to what they regarded as the true principles of poetic tradition, which had underlain the practice of all the great poets of the past – the Greeks, Chaucer, Shakespeare, Milton, and the anonymous authors of the old ballads. What they rejected were certain later developments of the poetry of the eighteenth century, which they regarded as corruptions of tradition. On the one hand there was the decadence of the limited classicism of the Augustans, with its stylisations of diction and its artificial restrictions of subject-matter. Wordsworth's dislike of these aspects of Augustanism lead him, perhaps, to do less than justice to the achievements of Dryden, of Pope, and of Gray. But he was equally, if not more, in reaction against other aspects of late eighteenth century writing, which literary historians have classed (along with his own work and that of Coleridge) as 'Romantic' or 'Pre-Romantic'. He protested against the 'frantic' Gothic novels of the day, against the imitations of German *Sturm und Drang* literature, and later, against the lack of real observation of nature which he detected in Macpherson's *Ossian*.

Against such affectations Wordsworth and Coleridge appealed to the truth of Nature and of the human Imagination. These two truths, for them, were essentially one, though for Wordsworth, the emphasis is on Nature, for Coleridge, on the Imagination. In the period of their most fruitful collaboration, Coleridge's metaphysical conception of the Imagination as the shaping force of the Universe, and Wordsworth's intuitions, received from his earliest years, of Nature herself as a living and a life-giving force, seemed to justify and reinforce one another. But in reality there was a fundamental divergence between their respective ways of looking at the world. This divergence was only to become apparent when, with advancing years, each was faced with the problem of how they were to continue to write poetry when the emotional impulses from which that poetry sprang became less and less frequent and less intense. That crisis is recorded by Wordsworth in his *Ode on Intimations of Immortality*. In this poem he sees himself as cut off from the Nature that had once inspired him, but he does not doubt that she still retains her life and her power; that:

> There was a time when meadow, grove and stream,
> The earth, and every common sight,
>> To me did seem
>> Apparelled in celestial light,
> The glory and the freshness of a dream.
> It is not now as it hath been of yore; –
>> Turn wheresoe'er I may,
>> By night or day,
> The things which I have seen I now can see no more.

>> The Rainbow comes and goes,
>> And lovely is the Rose,
>> The Moon doth with delight
> Look round her when the heavens are bare,
>> Waters on a starry night
>> Are beautiful and fair;
>> The sunshine is a glorious birth;
>> But yet I know, where'er I go,
> That there hath past away a glory from the earth.

Coleridge's *Dejection* is his reply to Wordsworth's *Immortality Ode*. In its original draft Wordsworth was actually addressed in it by name; only after the quarrel which sprang between them did Coleridge alter these passages so as to eliminate mention of Wordsworth. Coleridge, like Wordsworth, feels that he can no longer receive the imaginative stimulus from Nature that he once did. But for him, the vital source from which he is cut off is his own subjective Imagination. The beauty which he had realised in Nature was only a dramatisation of his human emotions:

> O Lady! we receive but what we give,
> And in our life alone does Nature live:
> Ours is her wedding-garment, ours her shroud!
>   And would we ought behold, of higher worth,
> Than that inanimate cold world allowed
> To the poor loveless ever-anxious crowd,
>   Ah! from the soul itself must issue forth
> A light, a glory, a fair luminous cloud
>   Enveloping the earth –
> And from the soul itself must there be sent
>   A sweet and potent voice, of its own birth,
> Of all sweet sounds the life and element!

This stanza expresses Coleridge's Idealist attitude, defined by his studies in contemporary German philosophy. The attitude is typical of nineteenth century (and later) thinking on æsthetic matters. It heralds one of the fundamental splits in the wholeness of culture, which was to lead to a progressive weakening, especi-ally in the succeeding Victorian Age. In this age, the practical activities of Science were dominated by Materialism, speculative philosophy by Idealism. Poetry and the arts in general were torn between the two – all of them being departmentalised, to their mutual loss. Under the influence of Materialism, Victorian poetry felt itself obliged to inculcate scientific, or utilitarian moral truth – as in much of Tennyson; or became preoccupied by minute and lifeless description of nature (Tennyson again), or a kind of painstaking historical-costume accuracy (as often in Browning). But the influence of an Idealist philosophy on poetry was hardly less harmful. The latter became subjective, formless, intellectually undisciplined, and abstracted from life into a world of dream and reverie. We see the beginnings of this already in

Coleridge's own poetry (such as *Christabel* and *Kubla Khan*)
The tendency is more marked in the work of Shelley and Keats
(whose *Lamia* is itself an allegory of the unresolved conflict
between Idealism and Materialism). By the end of the century,
with the Pre-Raphaelites, and still more the Aesthetes of the
'nineties, poetry had become something completely divorced
from the practical business of life – something namby-pamby
and a little shameful.

But Wordsworth's experience of Nature, in his most creative
poetry, was neither that or the materialist or the idealist. She
was neither a dead, mechanical cosmos, nor an imaginative
projection of the human mind, but an organic, self-existent
reality, from which the human mind itself drew its own power
and life. We may best designate his fundamental attitude as
Realism – using that term rather in its medieval, scholastic
sense (not in its later nineteenth century sense, which is practi-
cally synonymous with Materialism). The comparative failure
of Wordsworth's later poetry was largely due to his allowing
this Realism to fall to the level of mere Materialism – attempt-
ing to draw a prudential moral lesson from external Nature,
instead of accepting the whole of her potentialities, for evil as
well as for good. It was this which shocked Blake, when, after
reading *The Excursion*, he said: 'I see in Wordsworth the
Natural Man rising up against the Spiritual Man continually,
and then he is no Poet but a Heathen Philosopher at Enmity
against all true Poetry or Inspiration.'

But at his best Wordsworth's conception of the Universe has a
wholeness which it shares with the work of the older poets down
to the later part of the seventeenth century. The Cartesian revolu-
tion did much to destroy this sense of wholeness, and it is almost
lost to English poetry after Wordsworth's time, till it was
restored by Hopkins, and, perhaps, by some of our contemporaries.

The sources of this sense of wholeness in Wordsworth are to
be looked for, I think, in his countryman's background, with its
traditional patterns of life, and its pieties. Wordsworth was not
a peasant, like John Clare. But he came of solid North Country
yeoman stock, whose way of life was not so far remote from that
of the peasantry. He has often been accused of idealising, even of
sentimentalising, the Cumberland peasantry who play such a

prominent part, especially in his early poetry. Perhaps this was sometimes the case; but he often evinces an extremely shrewd insight into the less amiable qualities of the peasant – his meanness, his grasping hunger for land and small property. In *The Last of the Flock* he tells of the encounter with a farmer, who had once been wealthy, but is now carrying the last of the sheep he had owned to be sold. The man tells his own story, and how he was forced gradually to diminish his flock to save his wife and children from starvation:

> Sir! 'twas a precious flock to me,
> As dear as my own children be;
> For daily with my growing store
> I loved my children more and more.
> Alas! it was an evil time;
> God cursed me in my sore distress;
> I prayed, yet every day I thought
> I loved my children less;
> And every week, and every day,
> My flock it seemed to melt away.

The starkness with which these lines present the extent to which even the most natural of human affections are influenced by our material economic circumstances is in its way quite terrifying.

The religious background of Wordsworth's upbringing was that of an old-fashioned eighteenth century High Churchmanship, rooted largely in the works of such seventeenth century divines as Jeremy Taylor. But in the period of his most creative writing he had ceased to believe in the religion of his childhood. His real religion was that worship of Nature which finds expression in his poetry. This faith of his is often called Pantheism; but it would be more correct to use the term 'Pan-entheism'. This latter term implies, not the reduction of all things in the Universe to aspects of the Divine (which would be Pantheism properly so-called), but the doctrine that God dwells in and informs all created things, though he is transcendent as well. This latter doctrine is strictly compatible, as more extreme Pantheism is not, with orthodox Christian thought. Indeed, Miss Edith Bathoe, in her book, *The Later Wordsworth*, has pointed out that the famous passage in *Tintern Abbey* –

> a sense sublime
> Of something far more deeply interfused,
> Whose dwelling is the light of setting suns,
> And the round ocean and the living air,
> And the blue sky, and in the mind of man;
> A motion and a spirit, that impels
> All thinking things, all objects of all thought,
> And rolls through all things.

– closely echoes a passage in one of Jeremy Taylor's sermons, which, in its turn, is based on St Athanasius.

It might be said, in fact, that Wordsworth unconsciously transferred much of the sacramental thinking, which formed part of his traditional Christian background, to his attitude to Nature. For him, the Cumberland hills, and other objects of natural beauty, become vehicles of Grace, in the place of the Sacraments of the Church; almost, indeed, they become incarnations of the Divine. It is to the Christian mystical poets of the seventeenth century – such as Henry Vaughan (whose work he knew) and Thomas Traherne – and to the Christian Platonist Henry More, that we must go for the closest parallels to Wordsworth's religious attitude to Nature.

If we understand rightly this relation of Wordsworth to an organic tradition going back to the seventeenth century, it may be possible to take a juster view of his political development than some of his critics and biographers have done. Wordsworth has too often been represented as a youthful revolutionary who turned his back on his early libertarian ideas, and sought refuge in a reactionary Toryism. The episode of Annette Vallon, a French girl of Royalist sympathies, is, ever since it was unearthed a generation ago, usually dragged in here. It can, of course, be made to prove anything you please; but there is really no evidence that his love for Annette was of anything but passing significance in Wordsworth's development. Wordsworth's sympathies, it must be remembered, were with the Girondins, not the extremist party of the French Revolution. They represented the old, independent Republican tradition of the eighteenth century, whereas the Jacobins were much more like reformers and revolutionaries of the modern type. The Toryism to which Wordsworth later retired, was less an expression of reaction than an affirmation of the traditional pattern of society, based on land-holding, with its sense of the mutual obligations existing between landlord and tenant. It stood out against the enroachment on individual liberty of the Whig industrialists of the time. In his later years, Wordsworth retained his belief in the virtues of the free peasantry, and detested the policy of enclosures which was destroying the conditions which made a free peasantry possible. Though opposed to all ideas of violent revolution, he is recorded, at this period, to have expressed a large measure of sympathy with the aims of the Chartists.

Wordsworth's espousal of political traditionalism went hand in hand with a return to orthodox Christianity. The *Ecclesiastical Sonnets* express an ideal of the Church of England which forms one of the links between the old High Church tradition and the revived Catholicism of the Oxford Movement – whose Romantic theology owed not a little to Wordsworth's inspiration. These sonnets contain some not unworthy examples of his work, besides the wonderful *Mutability* – one of the finest sonnets he ever wrote. The decline in Wordsworth's later work has been very much exaggerated. It is undeniably cold – but it never sinks to the banality and vulgarity of which most of the Victorians, from Tennyson to Swinburne, were capable at their worst. But it is chiefly disappointing because it fails to develop the magnificent achievement of his earlier years. *The Prelude* remains a prelude only, without adequate afterpiece.

The truth of the matter seems to be that Wordsworth's Realistic conception of the Universe was born out of an older, organic and traditionalist pattern of society, which the Industrial Revolution swept away. A beautiful and little-known sonnet, written likewise in his later years, shows how Wordsworth was conscious that even the type of traditional religious faith with which he was most familiar belonged to a past order of things:

Oft have I seen, ere Time had ploughed my cheek,
Matrons and Sires – who, punctual to the call
Of their loved Church, on fast or festival
Through the long year the house of Prayer would seek:
By Christmas snows, by visitation bleak

Of Easter winds, unscared, from hut or hall
They came to lowly bench or sculptured stall,
But with one fervour of devotion meek.
I see the places where they once were known,
And ask, surrounded even by kneeling crowds,
Is ancient Piety forever flown?
Alas! even then they seemed like fleecy clouds
That, struggling through the western sky, have won
Their pensive light from a departed sun!

There is a sense in which the closing lines of this poem might
be applied to Wordsworth himself. It is possible to see him as
the last of the giants – the last truly great poet whose sense of
things was a unity; who was, in fact, a full man.

GEORGE WOODCOCK

Wordsworth and the French Revolution

I T I s difficult to consider Wordsworth's relationship towards the French Revolution without remembering the accusations of apostasy which were levelled against him, not only by extreme and ardent radicals like Hazlitt, but also by men of less engaged prejudices, such as Thomas Love Peacock, who pilloried the poet as Mr Paperstamp in *Melincourt*. The emotional reaction against Wordsworth is tipped all the more heavily since his leading denouncers were themselves men of such intellectual integrity that both of the critics I have mentioned were ready to acknowledge Wordsworth's importance as a poet even at the period when they most despised him personally. And when we add finally the dreary impression created by Wordsworth's cautious and pusillanimous character in comparison with the more colourful figures of his critics, it seems easy enough to follow the accepted consequence of giving a dog a bad name, and to assume that, however great a poet Wordsworth may have been, politically he was a scoundrel. But the case is too complicated for a merely curt dismissal.

Any discussion on this subject is in fact bound to be reduced in the end to an assessment of the motives for his change of opinion and allegiance. But in order to do this it is necessary to give in some detail the history of his varying attitudes and the circumstances surrounding them.

It seems clear that, from the first events of the Revolution, in 1789–90, Wordsworth took a sympathetic interest in what was happening in France, and when, in June, 1790, he started with Robert Jones on a tour of France and Switzerland, he seems to have gone with a mind predisposed to favour the revolutionary cause. Everything he saw emphasised his approval; in a letter to his sister Dorothy during this tour he told her that 'my spirits have been kept in a perpetual hurry of delight,' and re-marked of his arrival in France: 'We crossed at the time when the whole nation was mad with joy in consequence of the revolution

...and we had many delightful scenes, where the interest of the picture was owing solely to this cause.' His delight at this period was reflected in the *Descriptive Sketches* of this journey, written a year later, and in *The Prelude,* written more than a decade afterwards, after he had undergone most of his changes of attitude towards the Revolution, he could still recall his experiences with a renewed pleasure.

Though Wordsworth did not yet regard himself as a fully convinced partisan of the Revolution, he was sufficiently impressed by the picture he had received of France during this brief vacation trip to return in just over a year (November, 1791) for a longer stay. He passed through Paris, where he wandered in fascination through the streets of the revolutionary city; later, in writing *The Prelude,* he was to claim that the activities he witnessed moved him less than Le Brun's picture of Mary Magdalene, but, though there is indeed much evidence of Wordsworth's dubious æsthetic taste, it seems unlikely that he was in fact so impervious to the enthusiasm of the time and place as he later chose to claim.

His stay in Paris was brief, and he was soon in Orléans, in which city and Blois he remained until October in the following year, experiencing during this period two events which profoundly affected his personal life and also his attitude towards the French Revolution – his love affair with Annette Vallon and his friendship with Michel Armand Beaupuy.

Much has already been written and conjectured about Wordsworth's relationship with Annette, and I will discuss it only in so far as it impinges directly on his attitude towards the French Revolution. He first met Annette in Orléans in the winter of 1791–92; at this time he seems to have moved almost wholly in circles hostile to the Revolution, and the Vallons, like their Orléans friends, were all fervent Royalists, both Annette and her brother Paul being later involved actively in conspiracies against the Republic and the Empire. It therefore appears that, on first reaching Orléans, Wordsworth cannot have been very vocal in expressing his radical sympathies, since an extreme opposition of views on such a matter would hardly have provided a suitable atmosphere for a love affair with a young woman who shortly afterwards became so devoted a partisan of the reaction.

It was probably his relationship with Annette that drew Wordsworth to Blois, and here again he entered a reactionary environment, mingling with the officers of the local garrison, who were, almost to a man, anxious to employ their military ardours as quickly as possible in the renewal of Bourbon absolutism.

There was, however, one exception, Beaupuy, a young aristocrat of idealistic temperament, who had joyfully espoused the Republican cause, and who was anxious to take an active part in its defence. Wordsworth and Beaupuy soon formed a close friendship, and the arguments of the Frenchman soon re-awakened the poet's latent sympathies, appealing, he tells us in *The Prelude*, to his native English love of independence, and finally converting him to full support of the Revolution. It would appear, from the course which Wordsworth himself later pursued, that Beaupuy leaned rather towards the Girondins than the Jacobins.

It seems reasonable to suppose that this emergence of an important difference in attitude towards the Revolution may have been the beginning of the estrangement which later ensued between Wordsworth and Annette. It has been suggested that Wordsworth's later hostility towards revolutionary France may have arisen as a result of his desertion of Annette, in the form of a displacement on to an associated object. But Wordsworth can hardly have associated the Revolution with Annette, who was violently antagonistic towards it, and a case could certainly be made for a different course of development: that it was the disagreement over the Revolution that first provoked the rift between the two lovers, and, since Wordsworth's final abandonment of the *principles* of the revolution did not take place for some years, postponed a full reconciliation until it was too late. Afterwards, when Wordsworth finally entered the reactionary camp, the willingness of his action may well have been caused partly by a resentment towards the cause which had helped to thrust them apart and partly from a desire to assuage his feelings of guilt towards Annette by bringing himself closer to the cause for which she was an active agent.

Meanwhile, events in France, and the rise to power of the Jacobins, had complicated Wordsworth's position. His friends, the Girondins, were already passing into a steady decline of influence, and the Revolution, under the control of Robespierre and his associates, was beginning to assume a violent and dictatorial form which was repugnant to a man of Wordsworth's character. There is no doubt that the strained atmosphere, already loaded with terror, of Paris at the end of 1792, had a deep emotional influence on Wordsworth, and may have helped to provoke a reaction not shared by those who failed to experience the same direct impression. It would seem, from his remarks in *The Prelude*, that he at least thought of joining his fate with that of the Girondins; he still remained convinced of the justice of the Revolution itself, and it was only what he considered the Jacobin usurpation that he so far opposed. But he easily convinced himself that he

> ... both was and must be of small worth,
> No better than an alien in the Land,

and accepted the 'harsh necessity' of 'want of funds' as a good reason for his return to England. Wordsworth was, in fact, not the kind of man to make himself a martyr for any cause: as Professor Legouis has said:

A strange combination of outward circumstances and natural wariness always kept him from dangerous extravagances . . . He was not the man to defy fate. He it is who thought at one time of joining his destiny to that of the Girondins, but was prevented; who in the midst of the English counter-terror wrote a proud republican letter to the Bishop of Llandaff, but kept it in manuscript and probably never even sent it to his opponent; who in 1795 wrote satirical verses against the Court and the Regent, but decided not to publish them. His courage was of the passive rather than the active kind. He was capable of stubbornness and silent pertinacity, not of that fiery temper that hurls itself against the cannon's mouth.

Indeed, the only comment one might make on this view of Wordsworth's undoubted caution is that even his stubbornness was pliable when the need arose, for how else can we explain the difference between the steady collapse of Wordsworth's principles and the silent doggedness with which Godwin held on to his views through nearly four decades of moral persecution?

Whether Wordsworth returned to France again as a revolutionary sympathiser after the beginning of 1793 is a matter of conjecture. There is Carlyle's statement that he was present at the execution of the Girondin Gorsas in October, 1793, and the tale of Alaric Watts that on one occasion, either in 1792 or 1793, he 'decamped' from Paris 'with great precipitation', because he felt his life was in danger. But any such visit, even if it took place, must have been brief, and has left no trace in his own writings. The point remains biographical rather than critical, since the seed of his hostility to France had already been sown when he left Paris in the winter of 1792-3.

But the change took place by degrees which were imperceptible to himself, particularly since France was actually departing steadily from the revolutionary ideals of liberty, equality and brotherhood, and embarking on a career of internal repression and conquest abroad. His first impulse on returning home was to immerse himself in the writings of a philosopher who, in equating the revolutionary principle with an extreme individualism, suited Wordsworth's mood of revulsion from the centralising and authoritarian activities of the Jacobins. For almost two years from the publication of *Political Justice* in 1793, down to 1795, he appears to have been a fairly convinced Godwinian, and his abandonment of philosophic anarchism, celebrated in *The Borderers* (begun towards the end of 1795), is a reflection of the general disillusionment which began to undermine from this period that faith in the ultimate goodness and perfectibility of man which was necessary for the Godwinian.

On his return early in 1793, Wordsworth's attitude to the Revolution was still that of supporting Republicanism while disowning the actions of some of its advocates, and he was genuinely outraged by the English government's declaration of war in that year, regarding it as a wholly reactionary gesture. The Terror shocked him, but with the fall of Robespierre he saw a new hope for the aims of his Girondin friends. However, the Thermidorians disappointed him by adding to internal dictatorship the added crime of foreign conquest, which seemed tantamount to a renunciation of his and their ideals of universal freedom and brotherhood. Ernest de Selincourt has, I think, rightly, marked the end of 1794 and the beginning of 1795 as the time at which Wordsworth underwent the moral crisis which begun his renunciation of the Revolution and his return to a preoccupation with Nature, by its very origin escapist.

The rise of Napoleon could only attentuate further Wordsworth's Gallic sympathies, since he regarded the acts of the Consulate and the Empire as merely a further betrayal of the revolutionary ideal. Here, at least, Wordsworth has a case against Hazlitt, who was led away by his extreme Francophilism into supporting the dictator who gave the final death blow to the principal achievements of the Revolution, and there is no doubt that Wordsworth's sonnets protesting against Napoleon's various impositions, such as the renewal of slavery in the French colonies, written after the poet's visit to Calais in 1802 were inspired by a genuine hatred for oppression and of compassion for its victims.

It was after this time that Wordsworth's hatred of the Empire became mingled with a tolerance for the reactionary English government, which itself desired quite as strongly as Napoleon to destroy the achievements of the Revolution, and when war broke out again after the uneasy Peace of Amiens, he became a patriotic supporter of England. In this he performed in reverse the error of Hazlitt and his associates. The pro-Gallic faction saw only the tyrannies of the English government and thought that the only hope for freedom lay in the victory of Napoleon. Wordsworth and his fellow 'apostates' saw only the crimes of Napoleon and thought that the only hope for freedom lay with those who later became the architects of the Holy Alliance.

By gradual degrees Wordsworth allowed himself to be led into more and more open support of the English government, and, when in 1812 he accepted a political office for his services, his final corruption seemed sealed. As late as 1805 he talked of the revolutionary doctrines as 'creed that ten shameful years have not annulled', and castigated the Cabinet for its attacks on the radicals, but in later versions of *The Prelude* he was to show his growing conservatism by expunging these passages.

Yet Wordsworth remained *in theory* a radical, although his actions, motivated by interest, timidity, and more obscure personal emotions, steadily showed the opposite tendency. He never wholly renounced his revolutionary ideals, and dwelt even with some pride on the enthusiasm of his youth. When accused of apostasy, he replied in 1821, 'You have been deluded by places and persons, while I have struck to principles. I abandoned France and her rulers when they abandoned Liberty, gave themselves to tyranny, and endeavoured to enslave the world.' And there is no doubt that he really believed this, though he too was in fact deluded by places and persons. In the final event, though the position of Hazlitt was not so clearly logical as has often been held, his criticism of Wordsworth holds good. For ideals are of little use unless they are reproduced in action, and Wordsworth must finally be judged by his sycophantic support of one set of enemies of the Revolution against another, by his growing neglect to speak against evident injustice when it was practised by his own side, and by his willing acceptance of the position of an 'official' poet under an administration that persistently flouted the ideals he still claimed to hold. Perhaps worse even than the external treason was the inner disintegration it involved, and which cannot be dissociated from the steady desiccation of Wordsworth's poetical talent in his later years.

NORMAN NICHOLSON

Wordsworth and the Lakes

THERE was once a clergyman (tells Matthew Arnold) who, after saying how much he had appreciated the *Guide to the Lakes*, asked Wordsworth if he had written anything else. Such a story, even if it is not true, is not preposterous, for the *Guide* indicates the point at which Wordsworth's influence began to spread beyond the purely literary public. Much more than the poems it shows the way in which his thought was to help to modify the lives of the dalesmen. It is concerned less with the poet's attitude to Nature than with his attitude to Landscape, and as such it is of great importance in what one may call the tourist tradition in the Lakes, a tradition which is an excellent illustration of one aspect of the Romantic Movement.

The 'Description of the Scenery of the Lakes', which forms the main part of the *Guide*, was first printed anonymously in 1810 as an introduction to a book of drawings by the Rev Joseph Wilkinson. It next appeared, without the views, as an appendix to the Duddon Sonnets, and was published separately with a few additions in 1822 and 1823. But it was not till 1835 that it appeared in full form as *A Guide through the District of the Lakes in the North of England,* with notes added 'For the Use of Tourists and Residents'. This was the final form of Wordsworth's own text, but in 1842, with the poet's permission, it was edited and published by Hudson and Nicholson of Kendal. In this edition the original 'Description' is printed in full, but Wordsworth's 'Directions and Information for the Tourist' have been greatly enlarged by the editors till they make up about half the whole volume. In addition to these notes, there are three letters on the geology of the fells by Professor Sedgwick, together with diagrams of the mountains supplied by a Mr Flintock of Keswick, botanical notices from the blind John Gough of Kendal, and itineraries and distances taken from William Green's *Guide to the Lakes*. This Hudson edition was extremely popular and went through five or six printings, additions being made in several of them so that by 1853 there were five geological letters from Professor Sedgwick, lists of fossils and fresh-water shells, and also a chapter on the derivation of Cumberland place-names. These additions – which seem to have had Wordsworth's approval during his life-time – show two tendencies: first, a greater readiness to welcome the visitor and tourist to the Lakes, and, second, a new tolerance for the work of the scientist in the study of local natural history.

The first of these can probably be explained by personal -motives. Wordsworth was a Cumberland man, but he did not really belong to the people of the dales. As the son of the agent to an unpopular Lord Lonsdale, he must have been rather divided from the ordinary folk of Cockermouth during his earliest years. His stay at Penrith probably did little to change this, and it was not till he went to school at Hawkshead that he really got to know the dalesmen. That knowledge was intimate, and yet, in a way, it was deceptive. He seems to have been liked by the Hawkshead people, but he was never one of them. There must always have been the knowledge that his stay among them was temporary, that one day he would pass into another social stratum. This, of course, is what happened. He left Hawkshead, went to Cambridge, the Continent, and Alfoxden, and when he came back to settle at Grasmere with Dorothy, the old Cumberland society of the 'statesman' was passing away. Indeed, he had begun already to idealise the memory of it:

Towards the head of these Dales was found a perfect Republic of Shepherds and Agriculturists, among whom the plough of each man was confined to the maintenance of his own family, or to the occasional accommodation of his neighbour. Two or three cows furnished each family with milk and cheese. The chapel was the only edifice that presided over these dwellings, the supreme head of this pure Commonwealth; the members of which existed in the midst of a powerful empire like an ideal society or an organised community, whose constitution had been imposed and regulated by the mountains which protected it.

It is doubtful if the dales were ever quite like that, and, anyway, they remained so only in poems like *Michael*. The real dalesmen must have been a disappointment to Wordsworth. He seems to have known very few of them, staying as much a stranger at Grasmere as if he had come from Penzance instead of Penrith. Dorothy was fairly intimate with the village women, but it was the vagrants to whom her brother talked – beggars and pedlars, men whom he met and then did not see again, so that the impression they left with him was not destroyed by further acquaintance. It was natural, then, that he should turn for company to his more educated neighbours, most of whom, like himself, were settlers. He was becoming respectable; was married, had a comfortable income, and was more orthodox in his religion and politics. He was accepted, therefore, in the 'better' houses by people who sometimes tended to include the poet himself among the picturesque features of the district. In such circumstances the proud isolationism of Grasmere was gradually replaced by the benevolence of an old man doing the honours at Rydal Mount.

Tolerance of the scientist, however, was a more important symptom than tolerance of the tourist. For nearly fifty years the Lakes had been growing in popularity with connoisseurs of the Picturesque. Thomas Gray visited Cumberland in October, 1769, William Gilpin and Thomas Pennant in 1772, William Hutchinson in 1773. In 1778, Father Richard West published his *Guide to the Lakes*, designed for the tourist of taste and fashion, which directed him to all the best stations (or viewpoints) and told him exactly how to look at the scenes in front of him. Later there were many similar guides and itineraries, in which the authors copiously quoted each other, and improved and exaggerated the landscape, stocking it with overhanging crags and savage waterfalls, till it resembled more the scenery of Dante's Hell than of Wordsworth's Patterdale. Many of these travellers used the fells and lakes, as some people use music, primarily as a stimulus to their own emotions, and because of this they distorted the landscape in their own imagination in order that it should come up to their expectations of the romantic. The artists of the time, therefore, painted less what they saw than what they wanted to see, building castles on impossible crags, peopling the passes with banditti, and often dressing the inhabitants in tartan and plaid, since Cumberland was confused with Scotland in the minds of many.

It is obvious that for this sort of fancy-dress topography Wordsworth could have no sympathy at all. Yet, from one or two of the early travellers, notably from Gray and Gilpin, he did learn a good deal. These men belonged to the earlier phase of the Picturesque, before it had run wild into the Gothic. Gilpin, in particular, was concerned, less with the romantic associations of a scene than with its æsthetic qualities. From him Wordsworth learned to analyse a landscape like a painting, to consider the different effects of light in a valley or on a mountain, to appreciate gradations of colour and balance of sunshine and shadow. Many of the finest passages in the *Guide* show the habits of this sort of æsthetic scrutiny:

Days of unsettled weather, with partial showers, are very frequent; but the showers, darkening, or brightening, as they fly from hill to hill, are not less grateful to the eye than finely interwoven passages of gay and sad music are touching to the ear. Vapours exhaling from the lakes and meadows after sunrise, in a hot season, or, in moist weather, brooding upon the heights, or descending towards the valleys with inaudible motion, give a visionary character to everything around them.

But the æsthetic criteria by which Wordsworth judged the landscape were not drawn from the study of optics or geometry, but from Nature herself. He judged nature by nature. To Gilpin the landscape did not exist as a thing itself. He never really saw trees as trees or becks as becks; they were only masses of light and shade, foregrounds and backgrounds, angles, and perspectives and combinations of colour. Moreover, Gilpin had no doubt that, if he had been given the opportunity, he could have designed the show better than Nature:

In all these cases the imagination is apt to whisper, What glorious scenes might here be made, if these stubborn materials could yield to the judicious hand of art! – And, to say the truth, we are sometimes tempted to let the imagination loose among them.

By the force of this creative power an intervening hill may be turned aside; and a distance introduced. – This ill-shaped mountain may be pared, and formed into a better line. – To that, on the opposite side, a lightness may be given by the addition of a higher summit. –

Upon yon bald declivity, which stretches along the lake, may be reared a forest of noble oak; which thinly scattered over the top, will thicken as it descends; and throw its [*sic*] vivid reflections on the water in full luxuriance. . . .

It will proceed even to the ornaments of art. On some projecting knoll it will rear the majesty of a ruined castle, whose ivyed walls seem a part of the very rock, on which they stand. On a gentle rise, opening to the lake, and half-incircled by woody hills, some mouldring abbey may be seated; and far beyond may appear distant objects, under some circumstance of picturesque illumination.

Such fanciful tricks may be harmless enough as aids to the sketching visitor, but as an habitual way of looking at nature they are likely to become a dangerous and deceptive practice. Gilpin was always concerned with the general rather than the particular. His observations came between himself and the thing observed; he could not see the trees for the wood.

To Wordsworth it would have seemed almost blasphemous to regard a natural landscape *merely* as a picture. The æsthetic sensibility was needed, but it was only one way of trying to understand the complex and independent life of nature. Against the cult of the general he set up the precise observation of the particular, and it is in his skill in catching and expressing the essential particularity of a scene that he shows his true power of natural description. The large set-pieces of *The Excursion* are rarely successful, and even many of the wonderful passages in *The Prelude* are descriptions more of a state of mind than of the external world. But that world is evoked elsewhere with solid objectivity by picking out as in a spot-light one significant detail:

> [Let] The swan on still St Mary's Lake
> Float double, swan and shadow.

Or sometimes one or two such details are placed side by side and the result is a miraculously-built whole, a great sweeping outline which conveys more of the feel and touch and smell of the place than would a picture packed with minute notations. Such is the familiar description of Red Tarn on Helvellyn which Wordsworth quotes in his *Guide:*

There sometimes doth a leaping fish
Send through the tarn a lonely cheer;
The crags repeat the raven's croak,
In symphony austere;
Thither the rainbow comes – the cloud –
And mists that spread the flying shroud;
And sunbeams; and the sounding blast,
That, if it could, would hurry past;
But that enormous barrier holds it fast.

The most memorable of all his descriptive details, however, are those where at one and the same time, the object is created before us and interpreted in the poet's imagination. Then we find that its purely æsthetic qualities have an emotional value, while the emotions roused actually help us to see the object more clearly. Such a description is that of the green linnet in the hazels:

There! where the flutter of his wings
Upon his back and body flings
Shadows and sunny glimmerings,
That cover him all over.

And an even more subtle interdependence of object and viewer, eye and inner ear, thing seen and thing felt, is seen in the lines about the ash tree above Airey Force, that:

. . . in seeming silence makes
A soft eye-music of slow waving boughs.

It is not to be expected that there will be many passages of such intensity in the *Guide*, though the famous description of the lakes in October is as memorable as all but the very finest of his poetry, but in place of this we have many passages in which the æsthetic perception of Gilpin is combined with an objective (one might almost say, scientific) understanding of the scene:

I will take this opportunity of observing, that they who have studied the appearances of Nature feel that the superiority, in point of visual interest, of mountainous over other countries – is more strikingly displayed in winter than in summer. This, as must be obvious, is partly owing to the *forms* of the mountains, which, of course, are not affected by the seasons; but also, in no small degree, to the greater variety that exists in their winter than in their summer *colouring*. This variety is such, and so harmoniously preserved, that it leaves little cause of regret when the splendour of autumn is passed away. The oak-coppices, upon the sides of the mountains, retain russet leaves; the birch stands conspicuous with its silver stem and puce-coloured twigs; the hollies, with green leaves and scarlet berries, have come forth to view from among the deciduous trees, whose summer foliage had concealed them; the ivy is now plentifully apparent upon the stems and boughs of the trees, and upon the steep rocks. In place of the deep summer-green of the herbage and fern, many rich colours play into each other over the surface of the mountains; turf (the tints of which are interchangeably tawny-green, olive, and brown), beds of withered fern, and grey rocks, being harmoniously blended together.

This is both accurate and sensitive, and yet Wordsworth knows quite well that it is comparatively superficial. He is writing, as he says, merely *'in point of visual interest'*. Yet even within these limitations he is more perceptive than Gilpin, for where the latter could see only a 'very inferior' type of rock, Wordsworth notices screes and gullies which 'meeting in angular points, entrench and scar the surface with numerous figures like the letters W and Y'. The *Guide* is full of such observations:

The iron is the principle of decomposition in these rocks; and hence, when they become pulverised, the elementary particles crumbling down, overspread in many places the steep and almost precipitous sides of the mountains with an intermixture of colours, like the compound hues of a dove's neck.

We noticed, as we passed, that the line of the grey rocky shore of that island, shaggy with variegated bushes and shrubs, and spotted and striped with purplish brown heath, indistinguishably blending with its image reflected in the still water, produced a curious resemblance, both in form and colour, to a richly-coated caterpillar, as it might appear through a magnifying glass of extraordinary power. During the greater part of our way to Patterdale, we had rain, or rather drizzling vapour; for there was never a drop upon our hair or clothes larger than the smallest pearls upon a lady's ring.

[167]

(The last two of these quotations are imitated from Dorothy's *Journal*, which suggests that it was from her, or, at least, in her company, that Wordsworth learnt the art of minute observation. This may have been due partly to the fact that she seems to have had much the better eyesight.)

Now in all these passages it should be obvious that the æsthetic pleasure, though very real, is only accidental. The rocks, the bracken, the rain drops, were truly beautiful, but Wordsworth's joy was not so much in the beauty as in the rock, bracken and water themselves. What really mattered was that they were what they were. So that in the end it would not just have been impious to change the scenery for the sake of art. it would have been futile, for he wanted things to be *as they were*. This, to some extent was behind the conservatism of his later years, his prejudice against the larch, his dislike of alterations to buildings or gardens, his objections to the Kendal and Windermere Railway. But it also gave rise to a much more creative sentiment, something which we might call a respect for the land. It may be partly true to say of him (as Professor Fairchild has said [3] of Coleridge) that his 'soul submerged itself in the beautiful object, but only as a means of achieving a mountainous dilation which ultimately swells into a heavenly vastness'. Yet, though he may have made totems of the mountains, and may even have used them as symbols of his own spiritual aggrandisement, he never quite forgot that they existed in their own way, apart from and independent of the poet.

In the days of his full poetic powers this sense of the objective existence of the world prevented his imaginative vision from evaporating into the gaseous Gnosticism which is so often the end of idealism. In his later days, after the vision had left him, it provided one of the few reliable comforts of life. The 'light that never was' was gone, but the land was still there.

It was from this point, not from that of a half-understood mysticism, that Wordsworth's successors started. William Green and Jonathan Otley wrote their admirably factual *Guides*. The rocks, the plants, the beasts, and the birds were studied by local biologists, while the amateur antiquarian gave place to

[3] In *Religious Trends in English Poetry*, Volume III.

the expert local historian. No doubt there was a loss and a narrowing of vision, and, in some cases, the habit of tinkering about with grasses or stones or arrow-heads became an escape from responsibility in the present-day world. But at least these obscure natural historians were concerned with something that does exist; they were not just playing with their own imaginations. In their small way they were seeing one speck of the natural world as it really was, they were in touch with the true identity of nature. Today, the average townsman has lost all knowledge of that identity, and all understanding of his relation to it. His view of the countryside is based almost entirely on the distorted values of the Picturesque. He is laying waste the soil and turning the primary source of physical energy into his own destruction. He is, in fact, making himself an outcast in the world which has produced him and which – if it comes to the push – can get along without him only too easily.

G. S. FRASER

Common Speech and Poetic Diction in Wordsworth

WORDSWORTH'S greatness is unassailable. It will not, even to
his most fervent admirers, seem to consist in an unfailing deli-
cacy in his feeling for language or an unfailing tact and precision
in his use of it. No other English poet of his rank so frequently
startles us, in passages that ring right as a whole, with phrases
that ring wrong. A reader's feeling for the niceties of English
idiom might be tested, indeed, by the degree to which the last
word in this opening quatrain of a famous sonnet,

> The world is too much with us; late and soon,
> Getting and spending, we lay waste our powers:
> Little we see in Nature that is ours;
> We have given our hearts away, a sordid *boon*,

jars upon him. For one thing, the word means only more or less
and not exactly what it ought to mean. From the point of view
of the one who grants it, a boon is a concession; but the person
who receives a boon regards it as a benefit. And though we may
give our hearts away as a sordid concession, there will be no
real benefit to anybody involved in the transaction. The word
has been forced on Wordsworth by the scarcity of rhymes in
our language. It is not, certainly, really a recondite or pedantic
word; but it is something worse; after so many strong and plain
words – words that in sense and emphasis, and almost in order,
genuinely are 'a selection of the language really used by men' –
it is a weak and fancy one. It has a flavour of historical flummery
about it: 'Sire, I crave a boon!' A conscious artist in verse, like
Milton, or Pope, or Gray, or Keats, would have sacrificed the
whole quatrain, fine as it is, rather than use just that word just
there. For the weak and fancy word is not even tactfully glided
over; it is so placed, clinching the quatrain, that it draws the
maximum of attention to itself.

Wordsworth had higher purposes in mind than those of

conscious artistry; he thought that grand themes can carry themselves:

> ...Life, death, eternity! momentous themes
> Are they – and might demand a seraph's tongue
> Were they not equal to their own support;
> And therefore no incompetence of mine
> Could do them wrong.

Wordsworth was not exactly incompetent; he was, as I hope to show, the master of a range of styles which, if we consider the narrowness of his range of themes, is surprisingly various. He is the most diffuse, repetitive, and uneven of our greater poets; by no means, however, the most monotonous. What did wrong to his momentous themes was rather his negligence. These lines I have just quoted, with their slack Miltonic loftiness, have something of the false muscularity of the figures in a Flaxman drawing; in many settings they would pass, as one of those duller background passages that are necessary, in a long poem, to set off the high lights in the foreground. They seem singularly out of place, in *The Excursion*, in the mouth of a plain country parson. Wordsworth's failures in language are, in fact, very often failures of the dramatic imagination.

Of our greater poets, Milton is perhaps more of an egoist – it would be a question of nice shades on either side; but Milton's traditional topics took him out of the world of the self; Wordsworth's new romantic topics threw him back there. He is the poet of the self; when he is at his best, what he is nearly always writing about is the deep gropings of his own mind towards whatever sources of strength and joy it can discover. Yet his self remained, in some ways, a strangely blind one; blind to the existence of others, to the fact that we learn what we are through learning what others are; and even nature, quite in itself, is not properly Wordsworth's theme, but rather nature as sunk in the mind's own greater depths, nature in the perspective of the mind's needs. All this helps to explain his frequent and strange lapses of taste in diction. For language is a social thing (a sense of its finer living shades is not given to solitary brooders, but to lively talkers, like Byron, or receptive listeners, like Clough) and Wordsworth was a most unsocial being. When he loses the brooding self as a centre he can be quite shockingly absurd. Under the influence, perhaps, of the baneful geniality of Sir Walter Scott, he once attempted to rehandle the theme of one of the most beautiful of the Scottish ballads. One thinks of:

> I wish I were where Helen lies,
> Night and day on me she cries,

and of:

> None but my foe to be my guide,

and then one turns to Wordsworth's appalling *rifaccimiento:*

> Proud Gordon, maddened by the thoughts
> That through his brains are travelling,
> Rushed forth, and at the heart of Bruce
> He launched a deadly javelin. . . .
>
> And Bruce, as soon as he had slain
> The Gordon, sailed away to Spain;
> And fought with rage incessant
> Against the Moorish crescent.

Drabness is forgivable, but that is shoddy. It might seem typical of the dangers that Wordsworth ran as a poet when he slipped the tether that bound him to childhood memories and ruminative browsings on the Cumberland uplands. Yet there is *Laodamia:* a poem quite outside Wordsworth's usual range, a dramatisation of classical myth, and a masterpiece of conscious and deliberate verbal art. *Laodamia* perhaps convinces us, as Bruce and Gordon and Ellen of the Braes of Kirtle, these unhappy Balmoralish figments, do not, because she does not pretend to be a person in the ordinary sense; she is the sense of an atmosphere, the projection of a sentiment. There are, too, the political sonnets in which Wordsworth throws himself so vigorously into the rôle of an old-fashioned English republican who has become a new-fashioned patriotic Tory; yet, after all, that rôle had become his outward character. He could dramatise the effects of nature on himself, as almost everywhere; and states of feeling, as in *Laodamia*; and aspects of his own character, as in the political sonnets; but almost never other persons. If his use of language has an intermittent tone-deafness, it is because of the self-enclosure of his world.

Yet, if he could not be other persons, he could wonder about them. *Peter Bell*, for instance – a poem which on the whole seems to me to come off, in a way in which the comparable *Idiot Boy*, *Simon Lee*, and *The Thorn* do not – is a series of shrewd and absurd guesses at another person; Peter's twelve wives are absurd, but there are shrewd touches in the way a lonely landscape plays on his uneasy conscience; there is drama in the poem; but the drama is not in Peter, it is in Wordsworth's own excitement about him, in whatever it is – some queer complex of feelings never quite brought to the surface – that sets Wordsworth guessing. And in that undeniably great poem, in its much nobler but still comparable manner, *Resolution and Independence*, the drama is not in the old leech-gatherer himself – such touches as:

> a stately speech;
> Such as grave Livers do in Scotland use,
> Religious men, who give to God and man their dues –

have still an unconscious comical quaintness about them – but quite overtly in what Wordsworth projects into the old man, in a kind of consciously induced hallucination:

> The old Man still stood talking by my side
> But now his voice to me was like a stream
> Scarce heard; nor word from word could I divide;
> And the whole body of the Man did seem
> Like one whom I had met with in a dream....
>
> In my mind's eye I seemed to see him pace
> About the weary moors continually.
> Wandering about alone and silently....

What Wordsworth had met with, of course, what awed and terrified him in the old leech-gatherer, was a dream image of *himself*; of himself as a lonely, patriarchal, godlike figure. Wordsworth looked in men, as he looked in nature, for a mirror; for a satisfactory reflection, or phantasmal embodiment, of his own predicaments. The poetic shock that he felt – and that he conveys, at his best, with tremendous forcefulness – was that of unexpected *self-recognition*.

In all his best work, if one probes deep enough, he is talking to and about himself, and the self contains, it is not contained by, the visible scene. What is striking about his verbal art, and about his art generally, is the number of turns he could give to this endless monologue and to this perpetual exploration of the same inner scene. For he had started off in what, for him, was the most unpromising way, as the poet of a world outside himself, a poet of observation and reflection in the tradition of the eighteenth century; and what is notable, perhaps, about *Descriptive Sketches*, if one compares him with the last sound poet in that tradition, Crabbe, is the lack of exact detail in the observations and the vapidity of the reflections. This is the decaying heroic couplet at its most empty and mechanical:

> ...Is there who 'mid these awful wilds has seen
> The native Genii walk the mountain green?
> Or heard, while other worlds their charms reveal,
> Soft music o'er the aerial summit steal?
> While o'er the desert, answering every close,
> Rich steam of sweetest perfume comes and goes....

Such dead stuff, in the last two decades of the old century, was what ordinary cultivated readers meant by poetry. Naturally, they were becoming tired of it. It was a wonderful notion 'to choose incidents and situations from common life, and to relate or describe them, throughout, as far as was possible, in a selection of the language really used by men, whereby ordinary things should be presented to the mind in an unusual way'. The working out of the notion, however, was another matter. Poems like *The Thorn* and *The Idiot Boy* and *Simon Lee* will, to the ordinary modern reader, unless he approaches them with a very careful historical preparation, seem notable mainly for their clumsiness, their repetitions, their plodding emphasis on unpoetic detail:

> One prop he has, and only one,
> His wife, an aged woman,
> Lives with him, near the waterfall,
> Upon the village Common.

If Wordsworth had not the dramatic imagination, in the ordinary sense, neither had he, in the ordinary sense, the story-teller's gift. He was in some ways a very typical northern Englishmen; one can imagine him, with slow, burring speech, labouring out an anecdote in ordinary conversation, sparing no flat factual detail, and deliberately closing with the point of his story long after his hearers, in their imaginations, had passed it. He was aware, indeed, of this ineptitude himself. In two exasperating stanzas of *Simon Lee* he touches on it with a kind of surly apology:

> My gentle reader, I perceive
> How patiently you've waited,
> And now I fear that you expect
> Some tale to be related.
>
> O Reader! had you in your mind
> Such stores as silent thought can bring,
> O gentle Reader! you would find
> A tale in everything....

Quite so! But it is rather too much to be told – for this is the gist of Wordsworth's reproach to us – that if we were poets ourselves, we could do the poet's work for him. One would have to soak oneself dutifully in the very worst poetry of the later eighteenth century to feel, like Hazlitt, when he first heard these early experimental poems of Wordsworth's read aloud, 'the effect that arises from the turning up of fresh soil, or the first welcome breath of the spring'. For they must seem, to a modern reader, to imitate just those qualities of 'the language really used by men' that can never be transmuted into art: its garrulity, its repetitions, its confused goings back on itself, its flounderings. These early poems have preserved over a century and a half a queer, fumbling newness. There is still no context of the mind into which we can fit them tidily. They look, and are, wrong in themselves; but they were right – and Hazlitt, who was a sound critic, was right in feeling this – in liberating Wordsworth from dead themes and a dead manner. He did not go on writing in the manner of such things as *The Thorn*, because he had enough of the artist's instinct, if not of the artist's conscience, to recognise that this manner was a blind alley. But as he gradually left these attempts to imitate the naïve stammerings of rustic speech, and went on to acquire a stately and austere poetic diction of his own, that diction had been quite freed, at least, by his rash yet necessary experiments, of the stale mannerisms of the late eighteenth century.

That statelier diction of Wordsworth's has, as I have hinted, a surprising variety. I repeat: he is not a monotonous poet. His wider theory of poetic language, which allowed for many things, hardly allowed for the necessity in poetry of abruptness and concentration. Yet he can write, at times, with a concise tragic weightiness:

> My former thoughts returned: the fear that kills;
> And hope that is unwilling to be fed;
> Cold, pain, and labour, and all fleshly ills;
> And mighty Poets in their misery dead.

That theory hardly allowed either for the place of wit and humour (and the fine shades of tone that wit and humour facilitate) in poetry; yet he is capable, if not of these, at least of a sort of forcible invective, which such a predecessor in that genre as Dr Johnson would have admired:

> Shut close the door; press down the latch;
> Sleep in thy intellectual crust;
> Nor lose ten tickings of thy watch
> Near this unprofitable dust.

These lines have a quality Wordsworth is not often credited with, polish. And the beautiful *Extempore Effusion on the Death of James Hogg*, written in his old age, and sunk in his collected editions among so many obstinate prosings, has other unlikely qualities: grace, tenderness, an urbane melancholy, a Horatian tightness of phrase:

> Nor has the rolling year twice measured,
> From sign to sign, its steadfast course,
> Since every mortal power of Coleridge
> Was frozen at its marvellous source;

The rapt one, of the godlike forehead,
The heaven-eyed creature sleeps in earth:
And Lamb, the frolic and the gentle,
Has vanished from his lonely hearth...

Dipping into the formidable bulk of his opus, one comes again
and again with surprise on felicitous things he only did once.
There is *Poor Susan*, with its rapid subtlety of resolved ana-
paests, so different from his usual dogged iambics; with its
queer Blake-like vision of the country from London; and with,
perhaps, his *only* completely successful transmutation of the
words and thoughts of simple people into the language of art:

'Tis a note of enchantment; what ails her? She sees
A mountain ascending, a vision of trees;
Bright volumes of vapour through Lothbury glide,
And a river flows on through the vale of Cheapside...

She looks, and her heart is in heaven but they fade,
The mist and the river, the hill and the shade:
The stream will not flow, and the hill will not rise,
And the colours have all passed away from her eyes.

Wordsworth's fancy was, as Coleridge said, recondite and not
graceful; yet his one extended piece of fanciful writing, the
prologue to *Peter Bell*, has a rapidity and energy that recall – I
have stumbled on the comparison with astonishment, but it is a
just one, and in it must go – such early poems of Mr Roy Camp-
bell's as *Festivals of Flight*.

The Crab, the Scorpion, and the Bull –
We pry among them all: have shot
High o'er the red-haired race of Mars,
Covered from top to toe with scars;
Such company I like it not!

The towns in Saturn are decayed
And melancholy spectres throng them; –
The Pleiads that appear to kiss
Each other in the vast abyss,
With joy I sail among them.

[178]

And there is the conscious Virgilian art of *Laodamia:*

> Of all that is most beauteous – imaged there
> In happier beauty; more pellucid streams,
> An ampler ether, a diviner air,
> And fields invested with purpureal gleams;
> Climes which the sun, who sheds the brightest day
> Earth knows, is all unworthy to survey.

Wordsworth said of *Laodamia* that it cost him more pains than almost anything of the same length which he had written. *The Idiot Boy,* on the other hand, which is perhaps of all Wordsworth's longish poems quite the worst, was written rapidly in the heat of inspiration, and Wordsworth said that he had never composed anything with *more glee.* Should we wish that, on the whole, he had been a less spontaneous writer and had taken pains more often?

He had all the gifts of a very great artist in verse, except a persistent care for verse as an art; he felt it was better to say all he had to say – even weakly and draggingly, sometimes – than to say a little, and say it perfectly. And he has said more than posterity will listen to. There is too much slack stuff. Yet I suppose that he has left enough, written at the height of his powers, to justify himself. There are signs that he is coming in again (in my own student days, getting on now for twenty years ago, he was not much read or admired). In our own time, as in his – after that burst of political enthusiasm, rather like his own early enthusiasm for the French Revolution, in the 1930s – it is once again easier for the poet to retreat on his own inner strength than to cope with the world; and Wordsworth is the source, after all, of an unofficial English religion of natural piety and moral stoicism. He was a very great man and I do not begrudge him his return to fashion; but there are dangers, and I have tried to indicate them, in setting him up as a model of poetic style.

HENRY TREECE

Wordsworth: His Impact and Influence

1

OF ALL the major poets of the nineteenth century, none had a personality so unattractive as Wordsworth's, nor has had an influence so great on subsequent generations of English poets.

He has neither the intuition of Coleridge, the warmth of Keats, the gaiety of Byron, the daring of Browning nor the smooth craftsman accomplishment of Tennyson. The Vallon affair, which in another might have seemed evidence of humanity in Wordsworth appears vaguely shocking and even unmanly; his grand seigneur treatment of the importunate stranger at Haydon's immortal party has all the marks of caddishness; and one cannot help sniggering with Max Beerbohm at the beaky-nosed Bard as he stands in the driving Lakeland rain and condescends to pat a gawping country girl on the head.

We can laugh at him, even sneer at him, on a dozen counts – not the least being much of his later poetry – yet, when all the laughter has died away, Wordsworth still stands, a very great poet, and almost the only other to be placed with Milton beside Shakespeare. There have been many poetic talents brighter, more nimble, more likeable; but few, a very few, as massive in conception or in sheer bulk of achievement.

Wordsworth had to an extraordinary degree a quality which hardly another poet save John Clare or Robert Burns or William Blake possessed; the ability to remain in all essentials an ordinary man, untouched by those cultures and ideologies which normally lie outside the range or the desire of ordinary men. And here rests the secret of Wordsworth's honest greatness no less than of his triviality. The poet who draws always from within himself may top Heaven when he is young and strong enough to let life sweep through him like an unleashed flood; yet he may sink to the greyest Purgatory of pedestrianism as age overtakes him and his memories grow dim and drained of feeling.

Before I go on, it seems worth while considering in more detail two of the points I have already hinted at. The young graduate Wordsworth, a member of a respectable country family, with a likely though unliked future in the Church, went, burning with revolutionary ardour, to France in 1792. Quite inexperienced in politics or love, there he sustained two severe shocks. He found that when men have passed the initial stage of political theorising, their emotions sometimes drive them on to shed blood, so as to implement their theories, as happened in the September Massacres. He found also that when an ardent young man makes love to a young woman, it is not unlikely that he will get her with child, and that if he does, he will come up against a convention so strong that only a man of Shelley's moral calibre may break it without damage to himself as an individual. (It is perhaps interesting, though hardly relevant here, to notice that Shelley was himself born in the year of Wordsworth's indiscretion.)

It must be remembered that William Wordsworth moved against a strong background of peasant regularity, and obedience to established custom, and, moreover, that while in his native northern element he might appear more daringly advanced than his fellows, his rather unhappy mediocrity and loneliness at Cambridge gave proof of his actual callowness. France in 1792 showed him that he neither understood men nor women. He did what one would expect a frightened country boy to do in such a circumstance, and escaped from a world that would cruelly clip his wings back to the peasant world which he knew and where all loved him. And what is more he spent the rest of his long life escaping back, whether in Normandy, or the Highlands, or the Prefaces to *Lyrical Ballads*, or in that curiously disguised externalisation of his unhappy liaison, told as a sad story he 'had heard' in France; where, it is interesting to remark, the lover is of noble blood and his loved-one a plebian, a reversal of the actual circumstances.[4]

There are strangely divergent views expressed, even by critics of the highest reputation, on this phase of Wordsworth's

[4] *Vaudracour and Julia.*

life. Herbert Read, in *A Coat of Many Colours*, assumes with great force of argument that the effect of his love-affair with Annette was to produce in the poet a remorse so strong that it never left him, and which at last entirely consumed his talent. T. S. Eliot, on the other hand, in *The Use of Poetry and the Use of Criticism*, is just as sure that 'Wordsworth had no ghastly shadows at his back, no Eumenides to pursue him; or if he did, he gave no sign and took no notice; and he went droning on the still sad music of infirmity to the verge of the grave. His inspiration never having been of that sudden, fitful and terrifying kind that visited Coleridge, he was never, apparently, troubled by the consciousness of having lost it.'

Though I admire the courageous nature of Mr Eliot's assessment, I am on Mr Read's side in believing that Wordsworth did indeed become from this point onwards a man so desperately anxious to hide the skeleton in his cupboard that he ended at last by locking himself up with it. It is as though, conscious always of pain and guilt, he sought solace in God through Nature and through natural men, and expiation, among other ways, in making public, as in *Resolution and Independence*, the lot of the poor and afflicted. It is at these points, I believe, that Wordsworth becomes a prime influence for the poetic generations which follow him.

This desire to do something for someone is perhaps nowhere better shown than in the poet's letter to the politician, Charles James Fox, where he says: 'Recently by the spreading of manufactures through every part of the country, by the heavy taxes upon postage, by workhouses, houses of industry, and the invention of soup shops, etc, superadded to the increasing disproportion between the price of labour and that of the necessaries of life, the bonds of domestic feeling among the poor, as far as the influence of these things has extended, have been weakened, and in innumerable instances entirely destroyed.' And in 1798, six years after he had left the mother of his illegitimate child, Wordsworth, with his friend Coleridge, published *Lyrical Ballads*, where especially in *Goody Blake* and *The Idiot Boy*, we are shown with a vengeance how strong is the poet's desire to immerse himself in the life and problems and mental processes of the deserving poor. There is no revolutionary fervour, no self-gratifying lyrical outburst, no *Evening Walk!* Instead, in *Lyrical Ballads*, I recognise the beginnings of a self-mortification, moving in its very bathos, and especially moving since it points towards the way which at last leads to the death of the poet.

If this thesis is sound, then how might a way of thought and feeling, a type of poetic utterance, so dependent for their exist-ence on Wordsworth's private and even secret life have any influence on others whose experiences and necessities were, in the main, so different from his? Indeed, although *Lyrical Ballads* went into three editions by 1802, Wordsworth suffered a number of critical attacks, not the least of them appearing in the *Edin-burgh Review* when he was thirty-seven, an age at which it seems reasonable to assume his work, if it was to be successful, would have been fairly generally accepted. It is true that in 1823, when Wordsworth was fifty-three years old, Southey declared, 'Every year shows more and more how strongly Wordsworth's poetry has leavened the rising generation', and de Quincey in 1835 said, 'Up to 1820 the name of Wordsworth was trampled under foot; from 1820 to 1830 it was militant; from 1830 to 1835 it has been triumphant.' Yet is must also be remembered that even when Wordsworth was fifty-five, Alaric Watts tried in vain to find a London publisher who would take the risk of bringing out an edition of the poet's collected works.

The eighteenth century traditions of elegance and learning in poetry died hard. Only a man of Wordsworth's strong peasant constitution and energy, the mainspring of which was the remorse that at last destroyed him too, could kill them for a time. And even his best friend, Coleridge, who had been first with him at the barricades, using the language of ordinary men in a state of emotion, could not go with him all the way, since, as he says in *Biographia Literaria:* 'Wordsworth sinks too often and too abruptly to that style which I should place in the second division of language, dividing it into three species; *first*, that which is peculiar to poetry; *second*, that which is proper only in prose; and, *third*, the neutral or common to both.' And Words-worth's failure was apparent no less in his choice of the appro-priate image, as Coleridge also points out. In the 1815 edition of *The Blind Highland Boy* we have the words:

And one, the rarest, was a shell
Which he, poor child, had studied well:
The Shell of a green Turtle, thin
And hollow; – you might sit therein,
   It was so wide, and deep.

Our Highland Boy oft visited
The house which held this prize; and led
By choice or chance, did thither come
One day, when no one was at home,
   And found the door unbarred.

It is almost inconceivable today that in the 1807 edition, before
Coleridge had persuaded his friend to think again, the prize was
not the shell of a green turtle, but a washing-tub! It is not
surprising, therefore, that such a poetic vision was for a time
unacceptable to those who had been reared on Dryden and Pope,
and who only by an act of tolerance had come to admit the
poetry of Gray and Collins.

   Yet Wordsworth did come to exert an influence outside the
limits of his immediate literary friendships; not only on indi-
vidual poets, but on poetic tendencies in general; not only on
unpoetic individuals (like Sir George Beaumont, who presented
him with an estate), but on the State itself, which gave him a
Stamp-Distributorship, a Civil List Pension and at last the title
of Laureate.

2

Perhaps it would be most profitable here to consider briefly
some aspects of Wordsworth's influence on the course of the
English poetic stream, and first it is necessary to glance back-
wards and to see at what point he turned it into new channels.
I think that it may have been here:

   'Twas on a lofty vase's side,
   Where China's gayest art had dyed
   The azure flowers that blow;
   Demurest of the tabby kind,
   The pensive Selima, reclined,
   Gazed on the lake below.

that is, at the point of trivial, over-mannered Baroque elegance: a point at which the poet is saying hardly anything because the strict limitations of his art and the society in which that art was practised prevent him from saying anything, even if he had anything to say.

In its place, I like to feel that Wordsworth put:

> Our birth is but a sleep and a forgetting:
> The Soul that rises with us, our life's Star,
> Hath had elsewhere its setting,
> And cometh from afar:
> Not in entire forgetfulness,
> And not in utter nakedness,
> But trailing clouds of glory do we come
> From God, who is our home....

about which there is an honest breadth, a humility and a dedication of the self to the eternal verities, as far as man may see them. This poem shows a writer who at last has come to understand something of life and of men, in a way that the Wordsworth who wrote *The Labourer's Hymn* and the *Trepidation of the Druids* didn't. Moreover, it shows, if any single poem does, the moment at which 'Modern' poetry was born.

I like to believe that Wordsworth's influence in a forward direction is just as positive as it was in stemming the trickling flood of classical decay. A poetic manner, itself part of the *zeitgeist*, must not, if art is to survive at a higher level than that practised among Welsh and Icelandic bards, be allowed to outlive its day. It must, if it will not shift of itself, be taken outside and strangled, by some sensitive Barbarian, if needs be. And if the later Romantics, Tennyson and Swinburne, assisted by the sensuousness of their music (which in turn bred sensuousness of meaning) in sanctioning the Gilded-breast-and-Chrysoprase period of decadence, then it was the primitive Wordsworthian poltergeist who, with horny hands, clapped-to that Yellow Book and sent both Georgians and their Imagist opponents to the fields again.

Looking once more at those points in the 1913 Imagist Manifesto which say what the poets concerned intended, I do not feel that I have gone too far in this estimate: they wish

'To use the language of common speech....'
'To allow absolute freedom in the choice of subject....'

an estimate which is further supported by the performance of
T. E. Hulme in *Autumn*, and by Herbert Read in *Harvest Home*
or *Woodlands*, where a certain spiritual quality emerges from
but rises above the images of tangible things that lie on the page.

And, although I wish to establish no connection whatever
here with what has gone before, I am tolerably sure that until
the last year or two, the Poetry Society and its magazine, *Poetry
Review*, and all the poets and readers who grew up in the halls
of these institutions, were more subject to the visitation of
Wordsworth than to that of any other shade. This I mention
because I feel that Wordsworth's influence has been almost
unrestricted, and that he has worked diversely on diverse
schools and persons.

Naturally, if his influence is observable on poetry in general,
it must be observable in the work of individual poets. I believe
that three of the qualities which he introduced, or reinforced, in
poetry are responsible for the greater part of what we consider
good in letters today; they are, close attention to visual detail,
a rhythmic flexibility which controls and is not controlled by
form, and the courage to unbend if needs be into the vernacular
for the sake of greater verity.

Surely, such passages as the following:

> The honeysuckle, crowding round the porch,
> Hung down in heavier tufts; and that bright weed,
> The yellow stone-crop, suffered to take root
> Along the window's edge, profusely grew
> Blinding the lower pane. . . .
> The cumbrous bind-weed, with its wreaths and bells,
> Had twined about her two small rows of peas,
> And dragged them to the earth. . . .
>
> *(The Excursion, Book 1)*

> Have you observed a tuft of wingèd seed
> That, from the dandelion's naked stalk,
> Mounted aloft, is suffered not to use
> Its natural gifts for purposes of rest,
> Driven by the autumnal whirlwind to and fro
> Through the wide element?
>
> *(Vaudracour and Julia)*

freed poetry, so that Browning might write, in *Two in the Campagna:*

> The yellowing fennel, run to seed
> There, branching from the brick-work's cleft,
>   Some old tomb's ruin; yonder weed
> Took up the floating weft,
> Where one small orange cup amassed
>   Five beetles. . . .

and Geoffrey Grigson any one of a dozen of his botanical poems.

It is conceivable, too, that Wordsworth's use of speech-rhythms freed the pentameter once more, as Shakespeare had done at an earlier date, so that it might more tolerably be used as a philosophic and speculative medium. Although I do not believe that Browning considered Wordsworth as a Leader, lost or otherwise, in reality, I do feel inclined to believe that a deal of Browning's unrhymed work was made much easier for him to write because Wordsworth had released the poetic medium, which had been in chains during the Augustan period of letters. I think I would go even further, and express the opinion that T. S. Eliot's fine passage, from *Four Quartets*, is not un-Wordsworthian in its manipulation of a language more commonly associated with prose than with poetry:

> So here I am, in the middle way, having had twenty years –
> Twenty years largely wasted, the years of *l'entre deux guerres* –
> Trying to learn to use words, and every attempt
> Is a wholly new start, and a different kind of failure
> Because one has only learnt to get the better of words
> For the thing one no longer has to say, or the way in which
> One is no longer disposed to say it. . . .

It is hardly too much to say that the influence of Wordsworth on the use of common speech, on the liberation of metre, and on the way in which a man looks at the countryside has affected in various ways and degrees almost every poet writing in recent years, whether they will admit such an influence or not.

I shall not labour a point which I regard as being self-evident, though a few direct examples might not be out of place here.

Among the older poets whom I believe to have gained from
Wordsworth's existence are Hardy (*Weathers*), W. H. Davies
(*A Great Time*, and elsewhere), Herbert Palmer (*In Autumn*),
John Masefield (*Reynard the Fox*) and, perhaps best of all
examples, Victoria Sackville-West (*The Land*):

> Shepherds and stars are quiet with the hills.
> There is a bond between the men who go
> From youth about the business of the earth.
> And the earth they serve, their cradle and their grave.

Among the younger poets, there are Anne Ridler (*Winter Day*),
Esmé Hooton:

> . . . I thought that the gracious sky
> O'er-topping holiday weeks must yield a dew
> Fostering young shoot, young bud. And the blue
> Illimitable sky indeed topped the first instance
> Of dream lived, of two weeks long imagined; sun shone
> One glorious week, like a flower opened out the silk-soft scene.

> In Cumberland, where the hoarse cuckoo in that springtide
> tossed
> Echoing from hill to hill clear call; where bough
> Was burdened, the sward-comfortable vale embossed,
> With first leaf, with spring flower: where in a brow
> Formed vastly of sharp peaks the mountains ranged, where
> the sound
> Of waterfalls and music of mountain breezes
> Through rockfaults blowing, through the ear found
> Echoing passage . . .
> (*The Clerk's Spring Holiday*)

and Phoebe Hesketh:

> Now with the last light dying on the lake,
> I see the heron take his dark flight home;
> And remember the gypsy woman who once stared
> At tangled tea-leaves in a smooth white cup
> Until she lighted on a cluster spread
> Like a bird against the gleaming porcelain.
> (*The Dark Stranger*)

[189]

The influence of Wordsworth on the reader? I think that this might best be shown in a quotation from Herbert Read, one of the most exacting though liberal of critics, and one of the most dignified and precise of poets. He is writing of *The Prelude:*

I am continually aware of the presence of this poem; I have several editions of it at hand, and certainly there is no other poem in the English language to which I would so confidently refer my friends for that reanimation which only the best philosophical poetry can give us.

No other words seem necessary on the subject!

HERMANN PESCHMANN

Wordsworth's Poetic Philosophy

I AM aware that to write on Wordsworth's 'poetic philosophy'
is, at first sight, suspect: philosophy is not rightly to be defined
by such an adjective, nor is the phrase to be equated with
'philosophical poetry'. Yet it seemed the only brief, approximate
description of what I want to examine. I am not, in general,
concerned with the elements of systematic philosophy from
Bacon, Locke, of Hartley that here and there inform Words-
worth's work; though Hartley's influence is never negligible.
'The doctrine [Locke's] which derived all our knowledge from
the senses was capable,' writes Basil Willey,[5] 'of serving
Wordsworth, who imbibed it through Hartley, as a philosophic
sanction for his own most deep-rooted instincts, and furnished
him with at least a foundation for his own poetic theory.' That
is true. But, as he reminds us a few pages later, Wordsworth is
'representative of the modern situation – the situation in which
beliefs are made out of poetry rather than poetry out of beliefs'.
To appreciate this is to steer clear at once of Leslie Stephen's
claim to find a scientific system of thought in Wordsworth's
work, or Matthew Arnold's forthright denial of it. It is simply
to look elsewhere for Wordsworth's strength: to realise the
primacy of the poetic imagination over the rationalising intellect
in achieving the organic unity of his work. And in this specific
sense I think 'poetic philosophy' may be granted legitimacy of
nomenclature.

Wordsworth was a great poet for about ten years only:
1797–1807. This is not the place to debate Herbert Read's
persuasive theories to account for this [6]; nor the reservations of
the Wordsworthian scholars about them. The fact is indisput-
able; though it should never blind us to the number of fine poems
and sections of poems incrusted in the mass of pedestrian verse,
of inadequate emotive tension, marking the years after 1807,

[5] *The Seventeenth Century Background*, Chatto & Windus, 1946 (a).

[6] *Wordsworth*, 2nd Edition, Faber & Faber, 1949.

and increasingly after 1815. But in so far as a 'poetic philosophy' was (in the sense defined) adumbrated by Wordsworth, it was in the poems written, though not necessarily published, in that decade of his greatness.

Before turning to that period, however, we must glance at Wordsworth's instinctive, if impetuous and transitory, identification with the doctrines of William Godwin. Godwin's *Political Justice,* a pioneer work in the field of philosophical anarchism, makes Reason the sole arbiter and guide of conduct in politics or morals. From *Guilt and Sorrow,* written 1792–4, to *The Convict* (in *Lyrical Ballads,* 1798) or *The Ruined Cottage,* – composed, with its powerful anti-war sentiments, about the same time though later inserted in *The Excursion,* Book I – the influence is to be traced. Wordsworth had already found in Godwin's book support for the ideas of freedom and liberty he had acquired in France; but his final disillusion over the French Revolution, combined with his remorse over Annette, drove him to seek in Pure Reason an anodyne for all ills. His enthusiasm was short-lived. The melancholy story is soon told in *The Prelude,* Book XI, 223–320, of which these are the well-known key lines:

> till, demanding formal proof,
> And seeking it in everything, I lost
> All feeling of conviction, and, in fine,
> Sick, wearied out with contrarieties,
> Yielded up moral questions in despair.

> This was the crisis of that strong disease,
> This the soul's last and lowest ebb; I drooped,
> Deeming our blessed reason of least use.

That was the end of Godwinism; and in the same Book of *The Prelude* he tells how his sister, Dorothy, nursed him back to mental and moral health:

> She, in the midst of all, preserved me still
> A Poet

Book XI, 346–7

and with her,

By all varieties of human love Nature's self
Assisted, led me back through opening day.
Book XI, 350–3

Dorothy and Nature: the twin influences he acknowledges in *Tintern Abbey*. Henceforth, he was to live by a philosophy he learned not from books or men, but that came to him intuitively from, and found itself enshrined in, the poetry he wrote.

By the time he published in 1814 that chequered achievement, *The Excursion*, he saw, retrospectively, his poetic philosophy as a much more clearly elaborated and systemised coda than the wild, instinctive 'flashings of a shield' that so much of it was. He likened his whole work, in his Preface to *The Excursion*, to the form of a gothic church. *The Prelude* was to be the ante-chapel, *The Excursion* and *The Recluse* the main body of the church; his minor poems 'the little cells, oratories and sepulchral recesses [!] ordinarily included in those edifices'. If one smiles at this humourless grandiloquence it is yet not without point; and it is perhaps useful to maintain the simile and see the *Lines Composed Above Tintern Abbey* (1798) and *The Ode on the Intimations of Immortality from Recollections of Early Childhood* (1807), as pillars upholding the porch. Between the speculations of these two poems most of what Wordsworth was to expand and refine upon in *The Prelude* and elsewhere was already implicit.

Before we examine the poetry for its experiential philosophy we must be sure we understand something of what 'Nature' meant to Wordsworth; and must consider the generally accepted ascription to him of pantheism. Professor Willey in his admirable study[7] shows how, at this time, a state of physico-theology was developing in which religious emotions were being transferred more and more to 'Nature': personification and apostrophe was giving way to first-hand communication and apprehension of a religious or mystical kind. In the passage he adduces (*The Prelude*, III, 127 ff) the poet's consciousness of endowing inanimate nature with 'a moral life' is followed by the significant lines:

I saw them feel,
Or linked them to some feeling

[7] ' "Nature" in Wordsworth', *The Eighteenth Century Background,* Chatto & Windus, 1949 (b).

recalling at once their echo in *Tintern Abbey:*

> of all the mighty world
> Of eye, and ear, – both what they half create,
> And what perceive.

This is that disjunction between Man and Nature to which Herbert Read alludes [8], and on which he founds his theories that not pantheism but humanism was the real philosophy informing Wordsworth's work: a humanism that horrified Blake in *The Recluse* and that was incapable of reconciliation with Wordsworth's later Anglican orthodoxy. Myers long ago demurred about this usual ascription to Wordsworth of pantheism which normally implies an indifference to concrete details, a pursuit only of the whole. Mr Read is more explicit:

> Nature had her own life, which was independent of ours, though a part of the same Godhead. Man and Nature, Mind and the external world, are geared together and in unison complete the motive principle of the universe. They act and react on each other. . . . The exquisite functioning of this interlocked universe of Mind and Nature is for Wordsworth the highest theme of poetry; in poetry the process actually receives its final consummation. [9]

This is finely said. But it is not all. If the main region of Wordsworth's song is to be the Mind of Man, that 'discerning intellect' will only achieve what he prophesies for it:

> When wedded to this goodly universe
> In love and holy passion
> > *(The Recluse, 53-4)*

and Wordsworth is fain to

> . . . chant, in lonely peace, the spousal verse
> Of this great consummation.
> > *(idem, 57-8)*

Is not this the end of that disjunction Mr Read discerns? Out of the marriage of mind and the external world is to be born the

[8] Read, *op. cit.* pp. 134-6.
[9] *idem,* pp. 126-7.

new heaven and the new earth. Whether this should still be
called 'pantheism' is an open question. I think perhaps it might.
With our terminology perhaps a little clarified, we return to
the poems. To the early Wordsworth Nature was 'all in all':

> a feeling and a love,
> That had no need of a remoter charm,
> By thought supplied, nor any interest
> Unborrowed from the eye.
>
> (*Tintern Abbey*)

On this simple animism we need dwell no further; it is its
transformation into a theory of the creative mind acting upon
the separate, external world, and of their ultimate 'marriage',
that is important. Meanwhile, we should notice how it is on
characters thus 'married' to Nature, or on scenes that heighten
this sense of union, that he persistently dwells. Lord Clifford,
the Shepherd, is praised, in the *Brougham Castle* poem because:

> Love had he found in huts where poor men lie;
> His daily teachers had been woods and rills,
> The silence that is in the starry sky,
> The sleep that is among the lonely hills;

and the nameless boy evoked in *The Prelude*, V, 382-5 because:

> Listening, a gentle shock of mild surprise
> Has carried far into his heart the voice
> Of mountain torrents; or the visible scene
> Would enter unawares into his mind.

In *Resolution and Independence* the voice of the old Leech-
gatherer blends in Wordsworth's ear with that of Nature herself:

> But now his voice to me was like a stream
> Scarce heard; nor word from word could I divide.

And the whole reformation of Peter Bell is epitomised in his new
awareness of Man and Nature:

And now is Peter taught to feel
That man's heart is a holy thing;
And Nature, through a world of death,
Breathes into him a second breath,
More searching than the breath of spring.

(*Peter Bell*, 1071-1075)

It is a theme that Wordsworth never tires of. Sometimes he hints at the fusion in such exquisite lines as those from *Three Years She Grew:*

And beauty born of murmuring sound
Shall pass into her face;

or, in the heart-broken, last 'Lucy' poem, laments that fusion made absolute in death:

Rolled round in earth's diurnal course
With rocks, and stones, and trees.

From this sense of a bond between Man and the earth he loves, springs one of his greatest narratives, *Michael.* There is little explicit statement of this union in the poem, but it is pervasive of its every rhythm: the character of the old man partakes of the bare, austere, even awe-inspiring nature of his own countryside.

Returning to the 'pillars' of Wordsworth's 'gothic church', we find *Tintern Abbey* representing a spiritual stock-taking at the beginning of his great period, the *Ode* at its culmination – but blended in that poem with the pathos of realisation not only

That there hath passed away a glory from the earth

but that for him, personally, 'the radiance . . . once so bright' is

. . . now for ever taken from my sight,

– or, if not for ever, at any rate appearing at increasingly lengthy intervals. In a sense *Tintern Abbey* is, too, a retrospective lament:

> That time is past,
> And all its aching joys are now no more,
> And all its dizzy raptures.

But the richness of the poet's compensations, and the philosophic wholeness of his new experience compel belief in his 'abundant recompense':

> For I have learned
> To look on nature, not as in the hour
> Of thoughtless youth; but hearing oftentimes
> The still, sad music of humanity,
> Nor harsh nor grating, though of ample power
> To chasten or subdue. And I have felt
> A presence that disturbs me with the joy
> Of elevated thoughts; a sense sublime
> Of something far more deeply interfused,
> Whose dwelling is the light of setting suns,
> And the round ocean and the living air,
> And the blue sky, and in the mind of man:
> A motion and a spirit, that impels
> All thinking things, all objects of all thought,
> And rolls through all things. Therefore am I still
> A lover of the meadows and the woods,
> And mountains; and of all that we behold
> From this green earth; of all the mighty world
> Of eye, and ear, – both what they half create,
> And what perceive; well pleased to recognise
> In nature and the language of the sense
> The anchor of my purest thoughts, the nurse,
> The guide, the guardian of my heart, and soul
> Of all my moral being.

This is one of the supreme passages in all Wordsworth. Clearer, perhaps, than anywhere in *The Prelude*, we have that marriage of the mind of man with a sentient universe. But in the Immortality ode it is, somehow, impossible to believe equally in the worth of what is left.

> We will grieve not, rather find
> Strength in what remains behind,

is altogether too self-conscious a determination; and, magnificent poetry as the last stanza is, its philosophic consolations do not quite carry conviction. In the more explicit revelation of this mood in *The Prelude* (XII, 277ff) the truth is plain.

Professor Willey sees [10] in this Ode something of a denial of Wordsworth's central doctrine: that Nature needs no 'glory' from 'worlds not quickened by the sun'; and in his use of this mythological 'machinery' a contradiction of all his normal practice. The Fenwick note that he used this 'machinery' for a 'merely poetic' purpose lends weight to this criticism. Wordsworth, in fact, says Professor Willey [11], specifically affirms his habitual beliefs in *The Prelude*, V, 510-511:

> I guess not what this tells of Being past,
> Nor what it augurs of the life to come.

But although he is not there prepared to be explicit, Wordsworth *does* 'guess', for two lines further on he alludes to the child's first consciousness of the external world as being:

> that dubious hour,
> That twilight when we first begin to see;

the bright day already far spent. It is not, it seems to me, that Wordsworth is employing a thought alien to his central beliefs, but merely using an unfamiliar vehicle to express it. But his purpose here is different from elsewhere: not the memorable recollection of great moments of imaginative or mystical experience, but, as Professor Willey says,[11] 'an impassioned celebration of childhood as the period of most intense vitality, written by a man who realises that "the hiding-places of man's power" are closing.' Wordsworth still

remembers *how* he felt, but can no longer experience *what* he had felt.

There are many other poems that I would gladly linger over; but space is limited. There are, for example, *Expostulation and*

[10] *op. cit.* (b), p. 285 *et seq.*
[11] *idem.* pp. 285, 287.

Reply and *The Tables Turned*, positing their exaltation of 'a wise passiveness' towards Nature, and denouncing the ratiocinative mind and 'the meddling intellect' – traits which link them with *A Poet's Epitaph* and *The Prelude*, XIII, 207ff. Or the ameliorative effects of Nature, even in dire distress, a kinship in suffering, in poems like *Ruth*, *The Thorn*, and (despite the 'weak ankles' passage), *Simon Lee*.

I have scarcely referred to Wordsworth's political philosophy, nor supported my arguments with quotations from the famous *Preface*. The reason is simple: his politics and his criticism are covered by other writers in this book.

Many of my deductions about other poems, are made from the more explicit references in *The Prelude*, and in that sense, and by the citation of parallel references, it is pervasive of this study. No one can hope to understand Wordsworth's mind and poetry who has not read it; and who has not read with the closest care and attention such books as XII and XIII. But to me the genre of *The Prelude* is not primarily philosophic, but epic or narrative. There is no scaffolding of systematic belief clothed by the poetry and made integral to it, as in Dante. I would go further, and say that, for the most part, such philosophy as it does contain is not 'poetic' in the sense we have defined. Its beliefs were not being forged in the writing, but were anterior to it; contemporaneous with the past experience it records, and come to us, therefore, at one remove.

The Prelude, however, emphasises certain traits which we have not encountered elsewhere in our rapid survey and which must receive comment. Wordsworth always conceived of the poet, and himself in particular, as set apart from men as their teacher and harbinger 'Of joy in widest commonalty spread'. His *Preface* is instinct with it, and in at least two places in *The Prelude* he explicitly reaffirms it:

> But to my conscious soul I now can say –
> 'I recognise thy glory:' in such strength
> Of usurpation, when the light of sense
> Goes out, but with a flash that has revealed
> The invisible world, doth greatness make abode,
> There harbours;
>
> (*Book VI*, 598-603)

reverberating in *Tintern Abbey*, when

> we are laid asleep
> In body, and become a living soul;

the other, the well-known passage at line 334 in Book IV:

> I made no vows, but vows
> Were then made for me; bond unknown to me
> Was given, that I should be, else sinning greatly,
> A dedicated spirit.

Wordsworth habitually saw his fellow-men in their relationship to Nature; and the Eighth Book of *The Prelude* is sub-titled, a little priggishly, perhaps, 'Love of Nature Leading to Love of Man'; pointing on to his hopes of universal brotherhood explored in Book XI, and to his conception of his theme,

> No other than the very heart of man,
>
> *(Book XIII,* 241)

– a region he claims again as his own in *The Recluse.*

The Recluse itself – only a fragment of the first book in all – presents a problem to anyone dealing with Wordsworth's poetic philosophy. Written in 1800, though first published as prefatory to *The Excursion*, it was planned as a major work: the third, and one imagines the longest, section of a three-part poem to bear its name. *The Prelude* and *The Excursion* were the first and second parts. Why, then, were only 107 lines of a single book written? We can only conjecture. For this much is certain. Side by side with many familiar Wordsworthian tenets there is the formulation here of a creed that is no mere pantheism. Herbert Read calls it humanistic: '. . . the greatest exaltation of the mind of man that has ever been conceived.'[12] It is, in fact, atheistic; and as blasphemous whether from a Christian or a deist point of view, as Blake felt it to be. The language and the imagery recall Milton; the sentiments are such as Milton could have put into the mouth of no one but his Satan. Having proclaimed 'the individual Mind', subject

[12] *op. cit.* pp. 134-5.

To Conscience only, and the law supreme
Of that Intelligence which governs all,

he affirms his purpose:

> For I must tread on shadowy ground, must sink
> Deep – and, aloft ascending, breathe in worlds
> To which the heaven of heavens is but a veil.
> All strength – all terror, single or in bands,
> That ever was put forth in personal form –
> Jehovah – with his thunder, and the choir
> Of shouting Angels, and the empyreal thrones –
> I pass them unalarmed. Not Chaos, not
> The darkest pit of lowest Erebus,
> Not aught of blinder vacancy, scooped out
> By help of dreams – can breed such fear and awe
> As fall upon us often when we look
> Into our Minds, into the Mind of Man –
> My haunt, and the main region of my song.

The meaning seems unquestionable. Yet by 1814, when it was published, Wordsworth did not feel like that – if we can trust the evidence of *The Ode to Duty* (1805), the *Immortality Ode* (1807), or *The Excursion* itself. And so he could never finish it: its naked exaltation of humanity was incapable of reconciliation with either *The Prelude* or *The Excursion*, let alone with his later orthodoxy. Why, then, did he who so scrupulously guarded against the breath of scandal by excluding from *The Prelude* all mention of *l'affaire* Annette, publish this at all? And, moreover, in his prose Preface to *The Excursion* openly avow that the fragment he printed might 'be acceptable as a kind of *Prospectus* of the design and scope of the whole Poem'? There seems no answer. Yet, when an unknown Unitarian correspondent, after reading *The Excursion*, attacked him for not distinguishing between Nature as the work of God, and God himself, he is outraged! He says, 'a passionate expression uttered incautiously in the Poem upon the Wye' has led her into that error; and 'unless I am mistaken There is nothing of this kind in *The Excursion*'.[13] In truth there is little enough; but perhaps

[13] Letter published by Edith J. Morley: *Correspondance of Henry Crabb Robinson with the Wordsworth Circle*, Vol. 1, pp. 79-82. Quoted by Herbert Read, *op. cit*, p. 181.

the poor lady had never got beyond the prefatory fragment of *The Recluse!* The problem remains unsolved; but it does not seem to me one is justified, in the face of Wordsworth's outraged repudiation, in letting the doctrines of what after all *is* only a fragment weigh too heavily or disturb the balance of the philosophic structure of so large a body of his other poetry. *The Recluse* reveals the pitfalls into which his unsystemised beliefs could lead him; but almost everywhere else – except perhaps for an odd line or two in *Tintern Abbey* – those pitfalls were avoided.

When we come to the later poems it seems to me that what Wordsworth is trying to do is not so much to cover up his heresy, as Mr Read thinks, as to declare that ultimate fusion of man and nature as taking place in the supernatural realm of revealed religious truth. It is a belief to which Wordsworth had sincerely attained; but which, for the most part, he has failed to endow with *poetic* validity. His earlier aspirations were born of his sensuous and moral experience: of the impact of his whole being upon the external world, of Nature upon his total self. The poetry incarnating it was not the portrayal of a creed but the revelation of an experience; an experience inevitably at times, containing many minor contradictions. What the critics often fail to see is that its vitality lies in, or at any rate is testified to, by those very contradictions. When they were consciously resolved the emotion has become recollected in a shade too much tranquillity; revelation gave way to deduction; and the subsequent slackening of emotional tension nullified the poetry. It has not, however, it seems to me, nullified the beliefs informing it, nor proved its conclusions ultimately incompatible with the premises from which they slowly evolved. The poet of *Laodamia*, *Dion*, and the later poetry may have excellent things to say, and the poetry, on occasions, still reach a high level. But the fusion of 'felt thought' (Mr Read's phrase) is no longer apparent; instead of being born of the experience the 'philosophy' is pre-determined, and so, for us, second-hand.

Wordsworth, then was never truly a 'philosophical poet'; was never to fulfil Coleridge's great hopes of *The Recluse's* becoming 'the *first* and *only* true Philosophical poem in existence'. But he did, for one supreme decade, adumbrate, with all its inconsistencies and contradictions, a poetic philosophy that will hold the allegiance and command the respect, exalt the hearts and inspire the minds of all whose sensibilities have not become utterly blunted, or who can still envisage Reality outside the terms of a dialectical process.

'All in all,' writes Mr Read, 'Wordsworth's philosophy is a noble one, and because it was fashioned in an age of disillusionment, and in a mood of almost helpless despair, it is a philosophy that has particular significance for our own age.'[14] And not for these reasons alone. This is a moment when Wordsworth's rejection of 'pure reason' and his heedlessness of even a systemised epistemology is paralleled in the neo-Romantic movement in contemporary art and letters, and in the growing suspicion of the mechanistic answers to life's problems. Slowly men are awakening to a realisation of 'how small a part of all that human hearts endure' can really be ameliorated by economic means or by the centralised planning of the new technocrasy; that in the end 'the burthen of the mystery', the 'obstinate questionings' lie within men's own hearts and souls. I know of no body of literature not avowedly religious or proseletysing in aim, that is more likely to bring these things home to the average man than the poetry of Wordsworth's best years. It is a poetry that offers no cheap palliatives, but a deep consolation for the ills that human flesh is heir to, and

> In which the heavy and the weary weight
> Of all this unintelligible world,
> Is lightened.

It is a poetry informed with a philosophy in which we detect, if only fleetingly,
> a sense sublime
> Of something far more deeply interfused;

when for a brief span, but none the less surely,

> We see into the life of things;

and from which we return to our ordinary affairs and busy-ness spiritually nourished and mentally refreshed....

[14] op. cit. p. 188.

WREY GARDINER

Wordsworth's Prelude – *A Verse Autobiography*

DR JOHNSON thought that every man's life could best be written by himself, though what he writes can never be the same as the vision in the mirror held up by his friends and his enemies. Both are distorted, but nevertheless real, like a stick in water. And it is generally when an autobiography deals with the author's childhood and first beginnings that he most often succeeds in reaching the hearts of his readers. Wordsworth's *Prelude* is the greatest autobiography in verse in English, and Wordsworth's greatest poem. But autobiography is also an art and can be realised in many forms. To a poet it is not the exact record of the drab happenings common to all of us. He is much more likely to fix his attention on the memory of the view from a window when he first became aware of some deep spiritual truth, or the horrors in the prison of life before he had escaped from the wrong way of living. With a man like Wordsworth, who had dedicated himself to his art, and to the leadership of man to the highest level he can reach, it became an epic of which Wordsworth was the hero. He was perfectly aware that for a poet to talk so much about himself might lay him open to a charge of conceit, but he knew too, that self-examination of this kind in sincerity and humility can reveal to humanity the whole picture of its own glory and despair.

The Prelude is something unique in the literature of the world because it combines the epic power and range of poems like *The Divine Comedy* and *Paradise Lost* and *The Four Quartets* with the introspective voice of the writer himself, which the Renaissance had made possible. Montaigne's tower was not an ivory one. It was lined with books but it existed in a world where politics and the murder of the innocent in the name of outdated ideas were always round the corner. In *The Prelude* its author was discussing his own problems as being of the greatest importance, identified with the individual citizen who was also a sensitive person, a poet or a musician, who desired only to enlighten the darkness of his world with a little truth.

Wordsworth is often regarded as the renegade revolutionary who retreated to the Tory heaven of the Anglican Church. This may be partly true but his support of the rising radical movement of the Chartists in his extreme old age is generally conveniently forgotten. Wordsworth did retire to his native mountains to work undisturbed by the clash and sounding of the contemporary literary scene. *The Excursion* was the result, but how often the planned greatness we consciously aim at is only a vast ruin that has come to nothing and the work written under pressure of the hard world of youth something that has the freshness of immortality. *The Excursion* is dull and pompous, undramatic, tedious and ends with tea at the vicarage. Even Mr Eliot would have had a cocktail. *The Prelude,* on the other hand, lets us into a whole world of pure delight. It is a chaotic succession of events that the poet's mind has lit up with the rich glow of memory. But what is of the greatest importance is that the things he sees walking on his solitary road or the moon among the leaves of an ash outside his cottage window are of equal importance with the politics and the gaudy trappings of what most men think of as the more important moments in their lives. But the whole atmosphere of *The Prelude* is one of the freshness of experience remembered by a very great poet thinking about his past. In it Wordsworth achieves something that he never came near to in the often cumbersome sentimentalisings of his other work. And how much there was of it. Today it is difficult to think of those men who dedicated their lives to writing nothing else but poetry, who felt that a day had been ill spent if they had not a poem to show for it, or many lines of a great work in progress. Have we lost something very valuable in scoffing at these men's lives and ideals? Shall we be compensated by the mass of cheap articles, B.B.C. scripts and second hand lectures that our contemporary men of letters will leave behind them?

The Prelude has a message for future generations, a point that Wordsworth was trying to make. It recurs through the whole course of his work in fact. And that is one which is very modern, the influence of childhood on after life. Think back to your childhood, he says, as an explanation of the problems of your life. The child is father to the man. Modern psychology has no other lesson.

To many readers of poetry Wordsworth is too often remembered as a hypocritical old man of the mountains who wrote rather ridiculous poems about children lost in the snow, pet lambs, idiot boys and the minor wild flowers. It is true these are the people whose knowledge of poetry is chiefly derived from anthologies of short lyrics. His greatest work, *The Prelude* and *The Excursion*, are very long poems and they are in blank verse. When Wordsworth uses the rhymed couplet so hackneyed and soiled by his own century he is scarcely more than another Collins or Thomson but in these great monuments of blank verse it is impossible not to recognise the sudden thrill and splendour of great poetry.

Wordsworth put aside his first draft of *The Prelude*, but up to his seventieth year, knowing that it would be published after his death, he worked furiously at polishing it. Much has been made of the difference between the several versions of the poem. At seventy a man is naturally very far from the emotions of thirty-five and in fact an occasional pomposity does creep in; but it is too often forgotten that most of his emendations were stylistic and at least one amendment contained a couple of lines as great as anything he ever wrote. It was of the statue of Newton at Cambridge 'with his prim and silent face' to which the old poet added:

> The marble index of a mind for ever
> Voyaging through strange seas of thought alone.

In writing the autobiography of his first years Wordsworth meant only to introduce himself as the author of what he thought was the monument of his fame; *The Excursion*, that long dramatic poem in which the various aspects of Wordsworth's personality discourse interminably in the usual scenery. The nineteenth century however did not have the gift of dramatic writing which demands brevity and quick separated flashes of incompatible truths. But in *The Prelude*, which was written at a time when he had realised his own greatness but had not yet been spoiled by success and the habit of writing, he succeeded in creating a work of art that put him among the masters of autobiography like Jean Jacques Rousseau, those modern writers about themselves who were also breaking the chains of fettered humanity; and as a poet he can be hailed as the father of our own twentieth century poetry. For it is surprising how modern the diction of Wordsworth is, more especially in *The Prelude*. And how fascinating is his description of eighteenth century life, the country tavern, its door 'beset with chaises, grooms and liveries and within Decanters, glasses, and the blood red wine'. And the descriptions of eighteenth century London with its fairs, half rural Sadlers' Wells and 'negro ladies in white muslin gowns!' Wordsworth, like Baudelaire in *Imperial Paris,* was looking at life not in one aspect only, bounded by the mythology of a dead conviction, but in its truthful whole; from mountain cloud wreathing in the slow glorious convolutions of the eternal dawn, to the reality of the depths of city life and the gibbet swinging in the tragic countryside, full of beggars and various kinds of misfortune and death. It is perhaps because he sees with exact clarity that the modern poet holds the attention of his audience. Wordsworth had the peculiar power of seeing the common things of our visual world and making them eternally real with his diction which had the quiet exactitude of simple greatness. Nearly all his poetry came to him in the solitude of a country road. The road, in fact, recurs time after time in his poetry; the road, with the odd, tragic simple people he met on it, and his message of Hope and Love without which we cannot live. He spelt them with a capital. Today we hardly dare mention them at all. He

> Felt, that the history of a Poet's mind
> Is labour not unworthy of regard.

The great old man to whom we owe so much of our world and nearly all our language, lived through many terrors and many sorrows; but he lived long enough to be the stepping stone between the Renaissance world of Milton and Shakespeare and our modern world of Browning, Pound, T. S. Eliot, Herbert Read and the Romantic renaissance of the 1940s. From the cloud-bound fastness of his mountain roads he seems very much akin to us in our troubles today with his rugged individualism and last ditch defence of beauty and love.

> . . . By love subsists
> All lasting grandeur, by pervading love;
> That gone, we are as dust.

His struggle towards the independence of man, not the cipher of the economist but the lonely and the simple-hearted who ask only to be allowed to exist in their own world of beauty, will move us as long as *The Prelude* is read, that is, as long as we have a feeling for the incredible panorama of nature that in time must defeat the pettiness of all our centuries.

ROBERT GREACEN

Wordsworth as Politician

WORDSWORTH said to a friend in 1833 'that although he was known to the world only as a poet, he had given twelve hours' thought to the condition and prospects of society for one to poetry'; and again he remarked that 'every great poet is a teacher: I wish to be considered as a teacher or as nothing'. Nor should these statements cause much surprise except to certain æstheticians – who may wish hotly to dispute them – to whom diction and the technics of versification are by far more important than content. In tracing Wordsworth's gradual yet at some points perceptible swing over to a Tory mentality from fervent radicalism in early manhood, there will unfortunately be no place for an investigation of the general controversy of poet-philosopher versus poet-craftsman.

At the age of twenty, in 1790, Wordsworth set off on a trip to France with Robert Jones: they took £20 apiece with them and carried their necessities in pocket handkerchiefs. At this time Wordsworth was merely tepid with regard to republicanism; a sturdy-minded, independent Northerner, he had found Cambridge society novel and cultivated but not particularly exciting intellectually. Leaving the French 'mad with joy', in the early stages of the Revolution, he and his friend calmly went off to Geneva and Zurich. On this first visit to the Continent he was, to use a phrase recently current, an objective reporter. But in the interval before his next visit the following year, he allowed the first impressions to soak into his mind – and no poet made greater use of slow, intellectual reflection than the young Wordsworth.

In November 1791, then, passing through Paris, he listened to debates at the Assembly and the Jacobins' Club, pocketed a relic of the Bastille 'affecting more emotion than he felt', and became friendly with the ardent Republican Michel Beaupuy. When his new French friend pointed to a 'hunger-bitten' peasant girl and said 'it is against *that* that we are fighting' Wordsworth must have felt the thrill of allegiance to a noble cause. When Paris, in 1792, suffered shock and self-disgust after the September massacres, Wordsworth was himself infected to some degree with these emotions. Money at an end, he came back to England to publish the *Evening Walk* (1792) and *Descriptive Sketches* (1793). The latter, reminiscent of Goldsmith's *Traveller* outlines the harsh living conditions of the peasantry and expresses an eager sympathy for the defenders of liberty in France; it won him, incidentally, in 1794, the admiration of Coleridge who spoke enthusiastically of 'the emergence of an original poetical genius above the horizon'.

His political principles found still more energetic expression in a letter, then unpublished, to Richard Watson, Bishop of Llandaff, who in January 1793 had attacked the French Revolution. This reply shows how Wordsworth, while remaining in the English tradition of detesting bloodshed, sympathised with Paine's *Rights of Man;* and it gave him an opportunity of thinking out on paper his radical ideas.

This radicalism had in a sense been superimposed on a certain English moderation and scepticism of abrupt change; yet the early mood in which he wrote such lines as the following had no taint of hypocrisy, whatever his occasional private misgivings:

> But Europe at that time was thrilled with joy,
> France standing on the top of golden hours,
> And human nature seeming born again.

Coleridge was able to describe Wordsworth as 'a republican, and at least a semi-atheist', while he himself could put up such a defence (in retrospect) of free-love as this:

> Old Freedom was old servitude, and they
> The wisest whose opinions stooped the least
> To known restraints.

The outbreak of Anglo-French war set up a conflict that could never be finally resolved: Wordsworth the moderate but determined revolutionary confronted Wordsworth the patriot; Wordsworth the lover of Annette Vallon warred against the Wordsworth who was to take Mary Hutchinson to an English

altar. In August 1794, when he heard of the death of Robes-
pierre, while walking on the sands at Morecambe, he felt an
emotion of 'transport' and could once again indulge the dream
of the 'golden time'. But the war of self-defence perceptibly
changed into one of conquest; a qualitative change had come
about. Gradually Wordsworth, in order to maintain intellectual
self-respect, had to revise the more rigid earlier formulas: God-
win's revolutionary ideas had painfully to be abandoned, while
his sister Dorothy stood ready to apply the salve of domestic
comfort. (Women are normally less willing than men to suffer
for abstract 'principles', and when they are thus inclined tend
towards a relentless fanaticism). In the later 1790s he came to
view the ideal state as one in which the yeomanry could flourish;
and indeed Wordsworth never had a deep understanding of the
proletariat, rural or industrial, despite his sympathy for the
oppressed and 'the people'.

The final break with French ideals came when the Swiss
forest cantons, which had so enchanted him in youth, came under
French occupation in 1798. He described the parting of the ways
many years later in 1821:

I disapproved of the war against France at its commencement,
thinking – which was perhaps an error – that it might have been
avoided; but after Buonaparte had violated the independence of
Switzerland, my heart turned against him, and against the nation
that could submit to be the instrument of such an outrage. Here it was
that I parted, in feeling, from the Whigs, and to a certain degree
united with their adversaries, who were free from the delusion (such
as I must ever regard it) of Mr Fox and his party, that a safe and
honourable peace was practicable with the French nation, and that an
ambitious conqueror like Napoleon could be softened down into a
commercial rival.

Wordsworth's tract, in 1809, *Concerning the Convention of
Cintra*, which Canning is supposed to have considered the most
eloquent production since the days of Burke's polemics, was
written largely in opposition to the peace terms concluded with
the French in the Iberian peninsula by the British Generals
Burrard, Dalrymple and Wellesley. The brunt of the attack falls
on Sir Arthur Wellesley, although he was the most junior

General in command, and was only partially responsible for the Convention. The fight over the actual terms of peace is not wholly relevant; what is important is the affirmation by Wordsworth of the principle of nationality which was so largely to dominate (and later to darken) nineteenth century political action in Europe and that of the twentieth in Asia.

In a sense he anticipated Mazzini. Wordsworth, as an English patriot, felt himself called on to defend the national sovereignty of Spain and Portugal, and to protest against their somewhat high-handed treatment by the British Generals. The language of this pamphlet, laden with such phrases as 'the heart of the nation is in this struggle' and 'this just and necessary war', shows how far-reaching a change had taken place in his political outlook. About the same time he wrote a series of sonnets 'dedicated to national independence and liberty'. The wheel was nearing the full circle since those early days when he:

> Exulted, in the triumph of my soul,
> When Englishmen by thousands were o'erthrown,
> Left without glory on the field or driven
> Brave hearts! to shameful flight.

From now on the practical alliance with Toryism developed, partially aided by his keen interest in local politics; in 1818 he published addresses to the Westminster freeholders in support of the Tory party. Alarmed by the dark murmurs of discontent in industrial England he eventually came to approve of naked reaction, opposing Catholic Emancipation and believing that the Reform Bill would lead to what future Tories were to designate as 'red revolution'. In 1838 he even brought forth a sonnet – *Protest Against the Ballot*:

> Forth rushed from Envy sprung and Self-conceit,
> A Power misnamed the Spirit of Reform,
> And through the astonished Island swept in storm,
> Threatening to lay all Orders at her feet
> That crossed her way.

The young poet, noble and truly human in the expression of his faith in progressive ideas, passionately attached to social and personal ideals, became the author of work which the *Edinburgh Review* in 1822 could fairly accurately describe as:

a sort of prosy, solemn, obscure, feeble kind of mouthing – sadly garnished with shreds of phrases from Milton and the Bible – but without nature and without passion – and with a plentiful lack of meaning, compensated only by a large allowance of affectation and egotism.

Why did this change come about? Mr Herbert Read, always a critic to be treated with respect, has suggested that all may be explained by Wordsworth's affair with Annette Vallon and the subsequent need for rationalisation. That view, while undoubtedly attractive, does seem an over-simplification. Did this 'dedicated spirit', afraid of the logical consequences, both physical and psychological, of his own theories, turn to an anti-intellectual attitude because his faith was too brittle to absorb the impact of a horrible disillusionment? There are, we know, some natures so overheated in youth (of such 'impetuous blood') that they cannot sustain in maturity a balanced attitude towards their early ideals. Hazlitt, reacting to events in precisely the opposite direction, could believe Napoleon the incarnate spirit of liberalism – despite a mass of evidence to the contrary – and could mourn Waterloo as a disaster for the free and radical temper.

Moderate and sensible as he imagined himself, the shock of French tyranny was an inescapable blow for Wordsworth. He was unable to approximate, in political terms, to that wide, all-embracing philosophy which he stated with such memorable coherence in *Tintern Abbey:*

> I have learned
> To look on Nature, not as in the hour
> Of thoughtless youth; but hearing oftentimes
> The still, sad music of humanity.

Wordsworth, in this respect, stands in strong contrast to that poet whose spirit he so frequently evoked and beside whom, despite all his weaknesses, he occupies a secure place. Milton's whole being, and not merely his emotions, took sides; and having taken a stand he could not relinquish it without utter self-destruction. Nor can it be convincingly shown that religion claimed Wordsworth, however it was that eventually he became a defender of the Church of England. Religious orthodoxy, entailing no personal sacrifice – and guaranteeing respectability – cannot be considered religious faith.

Parallel changes in political attitude, brought about by much the same historical and emotional factors, have taken place in our own time. Substitute the year 1917 for 1789, the Russian Empire for France, the triumph of the Bolsheviks for that of the Jacobins; and, in place of the Napoleonic Wars, trace the history of ideas and the general tendencies of the last three decades. There have been many writers who, disillusioned with Stalinist Communism, now can find no good thing in Russia or in her Eastern European satellites. For them, as for their prototypes in Wordsworth's day, everything must either be rosy-fingered dawn or chaotic midnight. They have in a sense neither been able to control their over-enthusiasm nor deal sensibly with its inevitable reaction.

The purists may object that Wordsworth's tragedy was inherent in his early infatuation with the principles of Paine and Godwin; that had he stuck relentlessly to leech-gatherers in his youth, he would not have consorted with tax-gatherers in his age. In short, they contend that the *only* aim of the poet should be poetry, whereas this is true in a special and ultimate sense. One might equally insist that the object of a motor-car is to cover distance, proceed to explain a car's mechanism, and conveniently forget to mention that petrol is necessary to create the energy that will drive it forward. Politics, then – or political philosophy, to use a term that may be more generally acceptable – gave Wordsworth's youth dynamic purpose; that his later maturity was unable to produce an equally valid system of social and political concepts is not alone his tragedy but ours.

Despite his final turning to authoritarianism Wordsworth preserved, if in a peculiarly eccentric form, a strong love of personal liberty, a stubborn emotion that the English have always been loath to yield up to the harsh logic of events. In his prime there had been some difficulty in reconciling freedom with justice; and the same problem exists today, though one would have to state it in very different terms. Godwin had inverted the Rousseau thesis by saying that though man is born in chains the rational mind can count the links and through awareness of his limitations can discover a true freedom. In a memorable sonnet Wordsworth fused patriotism with the need for freedom:

> It is not to be thought of that the Flood
> Of British freedom . . .
> Should perish; and to evil and to good
> Be lost for ever.

Political philosophy, having served an early inspirational purpose, was the rock on which a great poet was finally shattered. Yet it is surely absurd to suppose that a consistently non-political Wordsworth would have left us a greater *corpus* of poetry. There were deeper causes of apostasy than mere material benefit, the one Browning suggested in *The Lost Leader*. The simple truth may be that, as we say nowadays, Wordsworth had written himself out before he was forty; and that, when he had exhausted those tremendous reserves of nervous and sensuous energy on which he had drawn freely in the golden years, the battery could not be re-charged.

PATRICIA HUTCHINS

Wordsworth's Prose

ALTHOUGH Wordsworth hurried to point out that poetry and prose were much the same thing – 'the same human blood circulates through the veins of each of them' – perhaps he showed his underlying attitude in making the antithesis between 'Poetry and Matter of Fact Science'.

Arguing that where prose is read once good verse will be repeated a hundred times, he deliberately reserved his best imagery for poetry, as 'the breath and finer spirit of all knowledge', the 'Impassioned expression which is on the countenance of all Science'. On one occasion he wrote to Crabb Robinson, 'Yesterday Mrs Wordsworth and myself were on the top of Helvellyn . . . I describe nothing of their appearances in prose, you will hear of them some future time in Verse.'

It is curious that Wordsworth, although he set out to use incidents and situations from common life and 'at the same time to throw over them a certain colouring of the imagination', never came to consider prose and its possibilities seriously. He made it serve as a means of explaining, to himself first of all, what he had written without philosophical or intellectual prejudice, poetry arising out of the fusion of deep thought and immediate experience. As a young man there seems to have been a possibility of his becoming a journalist, a career then without so much danger to the writer, and he would perhaps have passed on to criticism and essays, not that his subsequent work suggests that he was flexible or humorous enough to have made a great success of them.

Matthew Arnold declared that in poetry Wordsworth had 'no style' and when he sought one, fell into 'ponderosity and pomposity'.

As to his vehicle of expression in prose, as we must thus call it, this owes enough to the eighteenth century to have both dignity and balance. Although harmonious, it is intended for the eye rather than the ear. Throughout his life it remained very much

[219]

the same and if his characteristic form of sentence had been arrived at with difficulty (one thinks of George Moore's early gaucheness), once acquired it was only varied within certain limitations. Like a comfortably sprung carriage it travels along a well-made road in the right direction, sometimes increasing speed at a decline or rumbling rather weightedly along the flat, slowing up at some difficult hill of exposition.

There are times of course, when Wordsworth breaks all his own restraints, and his sincerity and feeling for words runs away with him. Arnold said of his poetry that there were passages when 'Nature seems to take the pen out of his hand, and to write for him with her own bare, sheer, penetrating power'; so something of this 'balance of profound truth of subject with profound truth of execution' is also to be found in the Prefaces to the *Lyrical Ballads*. There Wordsworth melted down the 'endless fluctuations and arbitary associations of language' as he puts it, and using factors then only quarter-known to literary experience, his genius introduced 'a new element into the intellectual universe'.

As the teacher he wished to be considered, Wordsworth had to make his own textbook. Coleridge had pointed out to him that 'every original writer, in proportion as he is great or original, must himself create the taste by which he is to be relished; he must teach the art by which he is to be seen; this, in a certain degree, even to all persons, however wise and pure may be their lives, and however unvitiated their taste. But for those who dip into books in order to give an opinion of them, or talk about them to take up an opinion – for this multitude of unhappy, and misguided, and misguiding beings, an entire re-generation must be produced; and if this be possible, it must be a work *of time*. To conclude, my ears are stone deaf to this idle buzz, and my flesh insensible as iron to these petty stings...'

If there had been less opposition to the early work and the wise and pure had not been so bewildered by this innovation in literature, perhaps Wordsworth would have written less in explanation and justification of his theories. We should then have been without his valuable statements as to the factors underlying the creative process as he knew it, his emphasis on the pleasure which the mind derives from the perception of 'similitude in dissimilitude' and its connection with intellectual and sexual energy, now being analysed in its physical and neurological aspects, the fact that pain itself is the other end of the same register. It is no wonder that Freud in his *Autobiographical Essay* mentions an aversion to reading certain philosophers and writers until he had arrived at his own ideas independently, and an important modern poet declared that he had taken good care not to read too much T. S. Eliot. Under large trees there is not much undergrowth and it is part of the equipment of every important mind to know when to stop being influenced or diverted by the attractiveness of another.

Leaving aside the autobiographical aspect of Wordsworth's letters and the interesting light they give on the period and his personal relationships, one can often consider them as preparation or expansion of his theoretical writings. For instance, to mention one passage alone, there is that account of his attempt to write in memory of his brother and how, by a curious reversal of mood, this failure enabled him to continue the poem on his own life, *The Prelude*.

For all his labour, Wordsworth's definitions have often been misused and partly quoted. There is the familiar *'poetry is emotion recollected in tranquillity'*, suggesting relaxation on a divan bed and plenty of cigarettes. This is the passage in full:

I have said that poetry is the spontaneous overflow of powerful feelings: it takes its origin *from* emotion recollected in tranquillity: the emotion is contemplated till, by a species of reaction, *the tranquillity disappears*, and an emotion, *kindred* to that which was [*felt?*] before the subject of contemplation, is gradually produced, and does itself actually exist in the mind. In this mood successful composition generally begins, and in a mood similar to this it is carried on....

Italics are used here to bring out the three stages described and to suggest that either due to Wordsworth's deliberate omission or the trick of some printer, the word *felt* has been left out. To illustrate the passage one might say that (1) Wordsworth undertakes an excursion and later remembers how much he enjoyed it. (2) He then begins to sort out the details, the unimportant and those which had been significant to him. (3) Gradually he begins to see it all again and with this his emotion returns. He *is* there; but as the poet this time, for as de Quincey says, 'it is not what the individual sees that will fix itself as beautiful in his recollections but what he sees under a consciousness that others will sympathise with his own feelings.' Thus something extra has been added to the memory of that emotion, and Wordsworth emphasises that during this process the mind 'will on the whole be in a state of enjoyment'.

As a matter of fact, there are several over-used figures of speech which say much the same thing – 'to go back to the time', 'to remember vividly', that is, *with life*, 'to be there in spirit' and to 'write with inspiration'.

When the intensity of that pleasure near to suffering which every writer experiences at some time, grew less in Wordsworth, and with it the ability to perceive contrasts, he did not make the transition from the poet to the book writer. He used his critical faculty upon the work of others only to illustrate his own theories. To read his prose is to be continually looking over one's glasses as it were, at his verse. Curiously enough, in spite of his interest in country people, there is no attempt to collect or reproduce special idioms or speech; there is nothing of Burns' interest in dialect or that impulse which sent Synge to the Arran Island. We have instead many of Wordsworth's simple characters talking the language of educated, unaffected gentlemen!

As Herbert Read points out, Wordsworth never came to a position by a theoretical approach. If Hazlitt found his feelings 'were deep but narrow . . . and his understanding lofty and aspiring rather than discursive' and although in Wordsworth's own words he wished 'Through the human heart to explore my way', as that critic declares 'he owed nothing but to himself'. Thus Wordsworth could never have walked, as a novelist, in another man's shoes. In his best poems, observation, sympathy with Man rather than with the idiosyncrasies of individuals, an extraordinary ability to convey the inter-relation between circumstance and place, climate and mood, were only made possible by the fact that he seems to have had little of the neurotic's variability.

Coleridge, revealing in half a sentence the difference between Wordsworth and himself, speaks of 'those accustomed to watch the flux and reflux of their inmost nature, to venture at times into the twilight realms of consciousness . . . and to feel a deep interest in the modes of inmost being.' Wordsworth, interested in species rather than mutations, did not probe in the same way. He looked outward a good deal, as though through a polished window. The supernatural in his work suffers from no adult table-turning: no words on the window pane for him. Both Burns and Scott, with something of the Celt's fear of denying the existence of fairy or phantom states of being, interleaved with our own, let their critical minds lie passive before folk beliefs, passing them on without making too rational a judgment. The Reformation never reached the recesses filled by beliefs thousands of years old; this has been left to the cinema and the newspaper. Perhaps Wordsworth's experience was more directly religious in the Protestant sense. He had simply 'been there' in the twilight regions, during the course of an imaginative childhood, and remembered later in phases of emotional tension,

> Feelings and emanations – things that were
> Light to the sun and music to the wind;

He complained that Dryden did not keep his eye on the object and on another occasion that words had become a substitute for things. There is something in Wordsworth of the small child's humourless stare, its determination to take in and thus own the image of the stranger or unknown phenomena as another possession of growing consciousness. Nor have his letters that intimacy with which Sir Walter Scott shared his moods with others, using numerous dashes and semi-colons and throwing in all sorts of ingredients for fun. When trouble drove Scott further in on himself, he still wrote of his diaries 'I walk with myself, I talk with myself'.

Yet in all fairness there are times when Wordsworth does let himself go. 'As to poetry,' he wrote in 1821, 'I am sick of it; it overruns the country in all the shapes of the plagues of Egypt, frog-poets (the Croakers), mice-poets (the Nibblers), a class rhyming to mice (which shall be nameless), and fly-poets (Gray in his dignified way calls flies "The Insect Youth", a term wonderfully applicable on this occasion).'

Like much of potted wisdom which needs to be re-earthed, examined again from time to time, there are also certain elements in thought and expression which have become too trodden down into language or literature; 'our smooth market coin of intercourse' as Coleridge put it. A poet's work suffers from the same effacement unless it is picked out and rehandled, polished up, even spat upon perhaps, and then passed into currency again.

If Pater pointed out that the fiction of his period carried a reflection of Wordsworth's work, many of our own writers may have forgotten this gate through which various tendencies passed, fanning out in different directions. Pater mentions Shelley's remark that Wordsworth achieved 'a sort of thought in sense' and D. H. Lawrence was to use bodily sensation to convey emotion; James Joyce, who practised poetry in order to write prose, also had to create the taste by which he was to be appreciated, simply by launching his work on what proved to be a very stormy sea. Virginia Woolf and others have also broken down the arbitary barriers between verse and prose and others now prepare to jump over them. 'The ancients,' Arnold declared, 'were far above us but there is something we demand which they cannot give', and in the same way a child is older, racially, than its parents.

DEREK PATMORE

Wordsworth and His Contemporaries

PROGRESS is a favourite word in our state-controlled society, and we are inclined to flatter ourselves about our ever-increasing culture. But if we look back at Wordsworth and his circle and study their lives and work; if we pause to consider the influence that this great poet had on his contemporaries, we may wonder whether we have the right to be so complacent. Has modern British literature any group of writers and poets comparable to that constellation of talent which surrounded Wordsworth? Samuel Taylor Coleridge, Thomas de Quincey, Charles Lamb, John Keats, and Percy Bysshe Shelley – they appear giants when compared with our present-day men of letters. And where is that nobility of thought and of sentiment which was so characteristic of these men?

The early days of the nineteenth century, admittedly, were bright with promise. The ideals of the French Revolution were still in the air, and many dreamt of freedom, equality, and the brotherhood of man. Society, too, had a respect for men of letters and the great aristocratic families of England still felt that it was their duty to foster and encourage genuine talent. We must not forget that the lives of poets like Wordsworth were made easy by the granting of official sinecures. As his friend, Thomas de Quincey wrote:

A more fortunate man, I believe, does not exist than Wordsworth!

Early in life, Wordsworth was left £900 by Raisley Calvert, a young man of good family in Cumberland, which enabled him to live with his sister, Dorothy, and to devote himself entirely to the writing of poetry. Then, due to the political influence of the Earl of Lonsdale, the poet was appointed to the sinecure of Stamp-Collector for the county of Westmoreland which brought in the handsome revenue of about £500 a year. Indeed, fortune smiled on this poet all through his long life and his last years were filled with fame and recognition. He became Poet-Laureate when Southey died in 1843 after the Prime Minister, Sir Robert Peel, had addressed him as 'the first of living poets', and his rare appearances in London were hailed as a social event. It was this combination of genius with success that made Wordsworth so remarkable a figure and it was one of the reasons why he made such a deep impression on his contemporaries. Wordsworth's triumph is all the more notable as he never made any concessions to his reading public, he lived apart from the rest of the world, and his own personality was not particularly attractive.

Wordsworth was fortunate in both his period and in his friends. He was lucky enough to be born into a cultured society which had wit enough to appreciate his unique quality and his verse appeared at a moment when English poetry needed new forms and new inspiration. Indeed, there is something Olympian about this poet – he seems to have stepped on to the contemporary stage from another world and his detachment was frequently god-like. If we examine this man through the opinions of his friends and contemporaries we will find that he often eluded and baffled them whilst retaining their admiration. Undoubtedly there is an awe-inspiring quality about a man who could write about his poems (then little appreciated by the public), as Wordsworth did to Lady Beaumont in 1807:

Trouble not yourself upon their present reception; of what moment is that compared with what I trust in their destiny? – to console the afflicted; to add sunshine to daylight by making the happy happier; to teach the young and the gracious of every age to see, to think, and feel, and therefore to become more actively and securely virtuous; this is their office.

We are inclined to consider Wordsworth as the central figure in a group of poets but this is an error. His contemporaries and critics often spoke of 'the Lake Poets', but in reality Wordsworth was apart from Southey and even from Coleridge. He was a lonely star around which others revolved and followed, and because he was a daring innovator, a reformer, and a Romantic, he became the acknowledged head of a new literary movement. Yet he remained isolated all through his life and few, except his sister Dorothy, really understood him. But even Wordsworth, unlike most modern poets, was an enthusiast. He was youthfully enthusiastic about the French Revolution and he was passionately stirred by Nature. Detached he might be but he lived in an exciting world.

Turning over the pages of early nineteenth century books of memoirs we realise the aliveness of this period in English literature. The personalities of men like Thomas de Quincey, Charles Lamb, and Coleridge, stand out clearly in all their charm, idiosyncrasies and brilliance. And who can fail to be moved by the ardour and fine enthusiasms of the young Keats and Shelley? And then perhaps we will wonder why such vivid and contrasted personalities were drawn to the solitary and somewhat egocentric character of Wordsworth. The answer probably lies in the fact that Wordsworth, although a revolutionary when young, was the most stable member of the Romantic Group. There was an orderliness and singleness of purpose about this poet's life which must have appeared very attractive to the opium-haunted Coleridge and de Quincey. His serenity must have calmed the gay-hearted Lamb, who was secretly tormented by domestic tragedy, and we know that both Shelley and Keats admired him as a great poet. Finally, Wordsworth's own poems reveal that he was capable of being a thoughtful and sensitive friend.

It is ironic that the three men, Coleridge, Southey, and Wordsworth, who were to be celebrated as 'the Lake Poets', first met in the West Country and that some of Wordsworth's finest poems were written in this district. It was during the summer term of 1794 at Oxford that Southey first met Coleridge. Robert Southey, a West Countryman by birth, was up at Balliol College. A student of Rousseau, young Southey was as revolutionary in his ideas as Wordsworth and he dreamt of founding an ideal republican settlement in far-off America. One day, a strange young man arrived at Southey's rooms with a letter of introduction. It was Samuel Taylor Coleridge, the younger son of the Vicar of Ottery St Mary in Devon. Whilst still an undergraduate at Jesus College, Cambridge, he had run away and enlisted in the King's Dragoons, and he had only recently returned from this escapade. At this period, Coleridge was 'a strange-looking youth, with masses of long black hair parted Miltonically in the middle, and so emphasising the expanse of a noble brow; open, luminous grey eyes; and a curiously large mouth, which, with its parted lips, looked weak in repose, but which, when it became the agent of the intelligence bespoken by brow and eye, uttered speech even then unparalleled in its fulness.' Such a romantic character was bound to appeal to Southey and when Coleridge showed enthusiasm for the former's American scheme they became fast friends. They left Oxford together and went on a walking tour of Somersetshire, and then Southey took his friend to Bristol. Here they both became engaged to two sisters, Edith and Sarah Fricker, daughters of a Bristol merchant, and before the year was out Sarah Fricker had become Mrs Coleridge and Edith Fricker had married Southey.

Meanwhile another young would-be poet was making a solitary walking-tour in the West Country. It was Wordsworth, who, after experiencing the deceptive promise of the French Revolution and a passionate love affair with a French Royalist girl, Marie-Anne Vallon, was now seeking consolation from Nature. Fate, however, was soon to join Wordsworth's destiny with that of the other two young men. It was in 1796 that the three poets first met. Wordsworth and his sister, Dorothy, aided by the legacy from Raisley Calvert, had settled down at Racedown Lodge in Dorset. This house belonged to a Bristol merchant named Pinney who had let it rent-free to the Wordsworths with the possibility that Wordsworth might act as tutor to his thirteen-year-old son. Because of this arrangement, Wordsworth often visited Bristol and it was here that he first met the 'two extraordinary youths' as he called Coleridge and Southey. It does not seem that Wordsworth saw much of Southey at this time, but both the Wordsworths were greatly taken with Coleridge. In 1797 they left Racedown and came into Somerset to be near the Coleridges. Soon the two poets were constantly in and out of each others houses and there began that remarkable collaboration which produced the *Lyrical Ballads*.

It was whilst visiting Coleridge at his cottage in Nether Stowey that the Wordsworths first met Charles Lamb, and thus another valuable friend was added to their small circle. Lamb had been an admirer of Coleridge at Christ's Hospital where they had both been at school and they had remained staunch friends afterwards. The intense intellectual life lived by this extraordinary group of friends is reflected in Coleridge's remark about the Wordsworths: 'We are three people but one soul'. And the part played by Dorothy Wordsworth, ever observant and sympathetic, must not be overlooked, for in an entry in her journal written during this period she wrote:

'William and I drank tea at Coleridge's. . . . Observed nothing particularly interesting . . . one only leaf upon the top of a tree – the sole remaining leaf – danced round and round like a rag blown in the wind.'

Dorothy's image later appeared in Coleridge's poem *Christabel* where he wrote:

> There is not wind enough to twirl
> The one red leaf, the last of its clan,
> That dances as often as dance it can
> Hanging so light, and hanging so high
> On the topmost twig that looks up at the sky.

These were halcyon days, and they show Wordsworth and his friends in their happiest light. Later, as the genius of these men developed, conflict entered into their personal relationships. Still, the nucleus of the English Romantic Movement was now formed. How did their work affect their contemporaries?

The *Lyrical Ballads* was extravagantly admired by the coterie of friends which surrounded Wordsworth and Coleridge but its sale was small. Even the later work of Wordsworth when he was at the height of his powers never commanded the popularity of Lord Byron's poems. Ironically enough the works of the now un-read Southey, such as *Joan of Arc* and *Thalaba The Destroyer*, were more attractive to the reading public, and the facile verses of the Irish poet, Tom Moore, were best-sellers. Readers still under the influence of the eighteenth century tradition and its stiff formality were not ready for Wordsworth with his cult of Nature and his poems about the humble of this world.

However, it says much for the society of the day that there were isolated young men who were quick to recognise the genius of Wordsworth and Coleridge. We all know Thomas de Quincey's eloquent account of his discovery of Wordsworth in his *Recollections of the Lake Poets*, and no modern film-star could have more adoration than that which this young Oxford undergraduate lavished on his favourite poet. Another young man of letters who worshipped at Wordsworth's shrine was P. G. Patmore, who wrote in his memoirs, *My Friends and Acquaintance:*

> It is very painful to me to put on record the personal opinions and feelings of Hazlitt respecting Coleridge, Southey, and Wordsworth, particularly as the two latter, men from whose writings I have received more delight and instruction than from those of any other two living men, or indeed from all others united, . . . men also for whose personal characters I have ever cherished a degree of respect amounting to reverence.

P. G. Patmore was an intimate of Hazlitt and a writer belonging to the Cockney School but this did not prevent him recognising the greatness of Wordsworth and it is known that he gave his son, Coventry Patmore, Wordsworth's poems as a model for a would-be poet. It is noteworthy that the early poems of Coventry Patmore are strongly influenced by both Wordsworth and Coleridge.

In 1816 the young Keats dedicated four lines of a sonnet to Wordsworth, and although he wrote to his brothers that Wordsworth had 'left a bad impression wherever he visited in town by his egotism, vanity, and bigotry', he always maintained that Wordsworth was 'a great poet'.

Shelley, unlike Keats, never met Wordsworth but the older poet undoubtedly had a profound influence on his work. There were definite affinities between Shelley and Wordsworth, and as one critic has written: 'They were alike as poets, in realising, conceiving, the Universe; and realising it as spiritual and *quasi*-personal. . . . They two, indeed, share, and share almost equally, the honour of giving to British literature a truly philosophical poetry, of conceiving for poetry the ideality and unity of the world, with the conviction of the theologian or the construction of a philosophy.'

Hazlitt, on the other hand, whilst admiring Wordsworth as a poet attacked him as a man and for political reasons. As his friend, P. G. Patmore wrote in his little-known study of Hazlitt in *My Friends and Acquaintance:*

With respect to Wordsworth, Hazlitt's estimate of him both as a writer and a man, was much nearer the truth than in either of the two other cases [Southey and Coleridge]; for the worst that Wordsworth had done in the way of political apostacy was, to accept an obligation from a party he despised, and thus cut himself off from the will as well as the power to use his pen against them. He never used it *for* that party; nor did Hazlitt accuse him of having ever gone a single step from the pure, even, and dignified tenor of his way, either to gain or to keep the good that he chose to accept from evil hands.

On the contrary, the worst that Hazlitt had to say of Wordsworth was, that he was a poet and nothing more; meaning thereby that he was incapable of taking any personal interest in the actual wants, desires, enjoyments, sufferings, and sentiments of his fellow-men; and that, so long as he could be permitted to wander in peace and personal comfort among his favourite scenes of external nature, and chant his lyrical ballads to an admiring friend, and make his lonely excursions into the mystic realms of imagination, and enjoy unmolested the moods of his mind, the human race and its rights and interest might lie bound for ever to the footstools of kings, or be half exterminated in seeking to escape thence, for anything that he cared, or any step that he would take to the contrary – . . . In short, Hazlitt seemed to look upon Wordsworth as a man purged and etherealised, by his mental constitution and habits, from all the everyday interests and sentiments with which ordinary men regard their fellow-*men*, and incognizant of any claims upon his human nature but such as have reference to *man* in the abstract; and that, while he could secure leisure to dream and dogmatise and poetise this latter theme, the living world and its ways were matters wholly beneath his notice.

Hazlitt was not the only one of his contemporaries who regarded Wordsworth in this light. Even Thomas de Quincey, after he got to know the poet well, had some acid comments to make about the idol of his youth. Yet Wordsworth was very patient with Coleridge when he began to disintegrate under the influence of opium, and no one could have been kinder to Coleridge's unfortunate son, Hartley. He also loved Charles Lamb and when the essayist died he wrote a touching epitaph:

To a Good Man of most dear memory
This Stone is sacred. . . .

Perhaps the highest contemporary tribute paid to Wordsworth was by his friend and neighbour, Southey, when he wrote:

> A greater poet than Wordsworth there never has been, nor ever will be. . . . I speak not from the partiality of friendship, nor because we have been so absurdly held up as both writing upon one concerted system of poetry, but with the most deliberate exercise of impartial judgment whereof I am capable, when I declare my full conviction that posterity will rank him with Milton.

Wordsworth, despite the fame of his last years, was never a popular poet but his influence was immense. How far-reaching were his teachings is illustrated in a lecture on Wordsworth which Frederick Robertson gave to an audience of working-men in 1853. He told them:

> The work he did, and I say it in all reverence, was the work which the Baptist did when he came to the pleasure-laden citizens of Jerusalem to work a reformation; it was the work which Milton tried to do, when he raised that clear, calm voice of his to call back his countrymen to simpler manners and simpler laws.

Today, it is hard to imagine that our modern society would allow so individual and detached a personality as Wordsworth to live in its midst. As we look back to those calm, promise-laden years of the early nineteenth century when England was still vigorous and young in spirit we may be grateful that Wordsworth and his contemporaries were granted happier times than our own. Perhaps, also, we can learn the lesson that great artists and poets need such freedom of thought and movement and peace of mind such as his contemporaries afforded a man whom they considered 'the first of living poets'.